ENDORSEMENTS

"As someone deeply invested in developing children's academic, social, and emotional growth, I am thrilled to see an inspiring and practical resource that educates and empowers teens to lead confidently in their school, community, and beyond. I wholeheartedly recommend this book for its thoughtful approach to teen leadership and the impact it will undoubtedly have on young readers."

—Holly Yarbrough, Founder of
Wonderstorm Leadership Academy

"Finally, a leadership book for teens that puts at the fingertips of any adolescent the mindset, tools, and strategies to imagine an extraordinary life and step actively into creating it and making a difference in our world. Coupled with a team of adults who believe in them, see them, and know they can create whatever they dream. Let's go!"

—Wendi McKenna, DPT, Transformational
Leadership Trainer for Teens and Parents

"This book celebrates leadership in all its forms, reminding us that real influence lies in our everyday choices and the impact we create for others. A must-read for teens ready to lead this next generation boldly, no matter their path."

—Katia Ravé, Transformational Leadership Trainer and
CEO of Impact Leaders, Ravé Strategy Studio

"This book offers an engaging and practical framework for our teens to recognize and cultivate their inherent leadership qualities and to lead with values of empathy, resilience, confidence, courage, and freedom. It is an all-in-one resource to invest in to support a teen in unlocking their unique potential, building confident communication skills, and developing a strong sense of self-awareness and vision."

—Keri Knudtson, Author, Speaker, Transformational Coach, and Founder of
Envision with Keri Consulting LLC

LEADERSHIP FOR TEENS

DISCOVER THE LEADER IN YOU

COMMITTED VISIONARIES

Copyright ©2025 Committed Visionaries LLC

ALL RIGHTS RESERVED. This book contains material protected under International and Federal Copyright Laws and Treaties. Any unauthorized reprint or use of this material is prohibited. No part of this book may be reproduced or transmitted in any form or by any means, electronic or mechanical, including photocopying, recording, or by any information storage and retrieval system, without express written permission from the author/publisher.

ISBN: 979-8-89079-267-9 (paperback)
ISBN: 979-8-89079-268-6 (ebook)

Committed Visionaries Publishing

DEDICATION

To the teens of today and the leaders of tomorrow:

We, the Committed Visionaries, dedicate this book to YOU—the present and future generation of trailblazers.

This book is an invitation to recognize the leader within, to own your unique vision, and to embrace your power at a young age. Our intention is to inspire, guide, and influence you to step boldly into your leadership, knowing that your choices today will shape a brighter future for all.

YOU are born to lead; choose to begin your journey today.

Life is NOW!

CONTENTS

Foreword
ix

Preface
xi

Introduction:
Get Ready To Lead!
xiii

What Makes a Leader?
1

Build Your Superpower
6

Communication is Cool
18

Solve it Like a Pro
31

Teamwork Makes the Dream Work
48

Take Charge of Your Time
66

Go With the Flow
83

Lead by Example
92

Make a Difference in Your Community
107

Your Leadership Adventure
119

About the Authors
125

FOREWORD

In a world where so many young people are searching for their place, it's all too easy to think, *I don't matter, My voice doesn't count,* or *Maybe I should just keep my head down and wait for things to get better.* These thoughts and experiences have become all too common among teens today, often fueled by a lack of confidence in themselves and their abilities. How did we get here? Why are so many young people just surviving instead of thriving and leading?

What if there were another way? A group of ordinary people bring extra to the ordinary, coming together with an extraordinary mission—to make a difference for the teenagers of today and tomorrow. Calling themselves "Committed Visionaries," they saw the need to empower young people with the confidence and tools to become leaders. And so, this book was born.

If only I had the chance to experience an emotional intelligence leadership program as a teen—it could have transformed the way I showed up, the choices I made, and the path I took. More importantly, it could have changed the way I connected with my family, friends, school, community, and even the world. Leadership is a privilege; it's a choice—not a right or something you automatically get. As a teenager, you hold the power to choose how you see and respond to the world.

I invite you not just to read this book but to immerse yourself in it. Take in the knowledge and tools it offers and the opportunities it opens. You are worth it. You are a gift. Your voice and perspective matter, and it's time to own your vision and value. You have so much life ahead of you, and you get to decide to step into your full potential. Don't wait another minute denying your worth, your power, or the impact you can make in this world.

How do I know this? Because I've been where you are. As a teenager, I felt lost, insecure, frustrated, and even afraid. I struggled to believe I mattered or could make a difference. Confidence was something I lacked, but as I started to believe in my potential, I realized that I was capable of far more than I had ever imagined. And just like you, I was full of potential and possibilities.

This is your chance to invest in yourself, uncover the leader within, and start building a life of purpose. I did it, and so can you. Now, it's your turn to soar—and to take others with you.

A life worth living is a life of giving.

—Michael Strasner

Author of *Mastering Leadership* and *Living on the Skinny Branches* and Worldwide Transformational Leadership Trainer

PREFACE

Welcome to *Leadership for Teens: Discover the Leader in You*, your guide to unlocking and being the leader you're meant to be. Whether you see yourself as a natural leader or are just starting to explore leadership, this book will guide you to embrace the qualities that set you apart and inspire others.

Leadership isn't about titles or control; it's about how you show up. It's about who you are, how you influence, and how you inspire by being authentic. As a teen, you have the power to lead right now, whether in school, your community, or among friends. Leadership is a way of being; it's not just what you do but how you carry yourself and connect with others.

At its heart, leadership starts with knowing yourself. It's about knowing your values, standing by them, and having a vision. This book teaches you to be a confident communicator, problem-solver, and team player. You'll explore resilience, adaptability, and how to be an example to others—not by having all the answers but by being true to who you are.

Each chapter offers insights and exercises to help you reflect on how to be the kind of leader who makes a difference, not just through actions but through your presence and mindset. You'll gain the tools to be a leader in any situation starting now.

By the end of this book, you'll have a clear sense of your leadership identity and the confidence to be that leader in your everyday life. Leadership is a journey, and it starts with you. Once you discover the leader in you and own the power within, you can choose to lead any team.

You were born to lead. It's time to be the leader you're meant to be!

INTRODUCTION: GET READY TO LEAD!

Why We Believe Being a Leader Rocks

Hey there! Ever think about what makes a great leader? Leaders are not just people in suits running companies or presidents giving speeches; they come in all shapes and sizes, and here's the truth: A leader is simply anyone who chooses to be one. Leaders are people who take a stand for something in life, whether it's big or small. Leadership isn't tied to a title or position; it's about taking action, stepping up when it matters, and making a difference wherever you are.

Leaders are everywhere. They can be found in school, standing up to bullies and ensuring everyone feels safe and included. We can spot them on the sports field, where leaders encourage their teammates to dig deep, push harder, and never give up, even when the game gets tough. They're in families, too—like the big brother or sister who steps in to help a sibling when they're struggling. Leaders are the ones who don't quit even when they fail; they get up, learn from their mistakes, and try again. Maybe you've noticed leadership in your teachers, coaches, or friends. And guess what?

Maybe you're already a leader; you just haven't realized it yet.

More than ever, the world needs young leaders like you, regardless of your age. Leadership isn't about being the loudest person in the room or having all the correct answers. It's about confidence and believing in yourself when no one else does. It's about courage and taking action even when you're scared. And most importantly, it's about knowing when to step up, when to lead a project, help a friend, or speak up for what you believe in.

Being a leader gives you the power to make positive changes in your life, school, and community. The juice helps you face your fears and rise to be the champion you are meant to be.

Here is the truth that you probably already know. The world needs leaders who stand up for what's right, unite people, and inspire others to be their best selves. Maybe that's you. Are you ready to lead?

Leadership: What's in it for You?

Why would anyone want to be a leader in the first place? Stepping into leadership is a powerful way to create a tangible impact on what matters most in your life, whether it's with your family, at school, or among your friends. However, beyond that, being a leader helps you live a life full of joy and meaningful connections with yourself and others. Leadership isn't just about helping others; it also comes with personal benefits. It enables you to grow and discover new strengths and gives you the confidence to take on challenges. Here are some individual benefits of living a leadership life:

- **Boosting confidence:** Leadership helps you believe in yourself. You'll start talking yourself up, smashing those self-doubts, and stepping into situations that might have once scared you.

- **Crushing fears:** Everyone has fears—even the most famous leaders—but a big part of becoming a leader is learning to face them. Courage doesn't mean you're never scared; it means you go for it even when you are.

- **Making smart decisions:** When you lead, you learn to make choices that help you and positively impact the people around you. Imagine being the go-to person for making intelligent moves.

- **Creating positive change:** Whether organizing a school event, starting a community project, or helping a friend in need, leadership allows you to step up and make a difference. You can be the person who helps make your school and community better.

You might think leadership is something for later in life, but trust me, it's not! Leaders come in all ages, and teen leaders bring fresh ideas, energy, and the drive to shake things up. You're probably already practicing leadership every day without even realizing it. Leadership shows up in many ways, such as helping a friend, standing up for what's right, doing the right thing when no one's watching, or simply believing in yourself when times get tough. This book will help you recognize and grow those leadership skills, giving you the confidence to take them to the next level.

This book was created by a group of leaders who came together with a shared goal: to inspire more leadership in the world. Our mission is to awaken the leader within you and give you the tools to strengthen that leadership muscle. We want to empower you to live boldly, go after your dreams, and create a life you truly love.

Are you ready to dive in and unlock the leader that's already inside you?

Before you dive into this book to discover the leader in you, there's something essential you need to understand about leadership: It all starts with vision. And no, it is not about what you see with your eyes. It's about the big-picture idea of where you want your life to go. Your vision is the personal roadmap for your future starting now, so let's take a moment to get curious about what really matters to you.

Vision: Your Compass to Leadership
By Valery B Ireland

Imagine you're holding a GPS that can guide you through the twists and turns of life. Now, instead of typing in an address, what if you could set a destination for your future: where you want to go, who you want to become, and what kind of impact you want to have? That's the power of vision. It's like a personal compass, showing you the way even when the road ahead seems uncertain.

What exactly is a vision, and why is it so important? A vision isn't just about having goals or daydreaming about what life could be. It's about bringing the future into the present. It's about imagining what you want your life to look like and then making intentional choices to get there. Whether your vision is about your family, studies, career, or the change you want to create in the world, it's a force that drives you forward.

Have you ever asked yourself:

- What do I truly love?
- What makes me excited to get out of bed in the morning?
- What impact do I want to leave on the world, my friends, or even just one person or yourself?
- What's missing in my life, and how can I create it?

These questions hold the key to uncovering your vision. Here's the thing: Your vision doesn't have to be something huge, like saving the world (although it totally can be). Sometimes, it's about something small but powerful, like being more confident, helping others, being kind and mindful to others, or mastering a skill you're passionate about.

In a constantly changing world, where everyone seems to have an opinion about what you should do, having a vision gives you clarity. Your vision is like a filter for all the noise, helping you see what truly matters to you and what doesn't. When you have a vision, you stop living life with eyes, ears, and heart half closed, aimlessly following the crowd, and you start making intentional decisions that bring you closer to your goals.

A powerful vision isn't just a wish or a nice idea. It's something you commit to and makes you excited to take action every single day. Your vision doesn't have to be set in stone. It can shift, grow, and evolve as you do. The key is to start with the end in mind and let that vision guide your choices, no matter how big or small. As you grow, new aspects will be added, and your vision will expand to new levels that will work even better for you in the long run.

Here are some questions to ask yourself to increase your curiosity:

What would life look like if you stopped leaving things to chance and instead created a clear intention for what you want?

_____
_____
_____

What could you achieve if you believed your vision was possible even before it happened?

_____
_____
_____

Who would you have to be to make your vision a reality?

_____
_____
_____

Your vision is like a magnet; it pulls you toward what's possible. And the amazing thing is, when you live with vision, it becomes contagious. Your excitement, passion, confidence, and purpose will inspire others to find their vision or to join yours, creating a bigger, positive impact in the world.

As you begin to explore your vision, remember this: Everything starts with vision (a desire) and ends with vision (a goal). Whether it's a small daily goal or a life-changing mission, your leadership begins by seeing the future you want to create and taking action to make it real.

Picture this:

What if you had a clear vision that gave you the confidence to tackle any difficult situation?

What if you knew exactly what you wanted to do and started making small (or large) steps toward it today?

How would it feel to inspire others (and yourself) by purposefully living out your vision?

Vision isn't about having everything figured out right now. It starts by asking yourself:

What gets me excited?

What's something I can't stop thinking about doing?

What do I wish I could change in the world or in my school or community?

Once you explore these questions, you'll start shaping your vision. When you have that vision, it acts like your compass, your built-in GPS. The more you go after that vision, the more your inner GPS guides you, and the more doors will open to support your vision. Your vision helps you make better choices, take the right steps, lead purposefully, and create the change you wish to see.

Ask yourself:

What's my vision?

_____

_____

_____

Who do I want to be?

_____

_____

_____

What's the next step I can take to get there?

_____

_____

_____

In leadership—and in life—vision is what sets you apart. It's the spark that turns ideas into action and dreams into reality. And here's the best part: Your vision can be whatever you want it to be. Big or small, personal or global, it's your unique blueprint for how you want to be and live.

Without a clear sense of where you're headed, it's easy to get distracted and follow someone else's path instead of creating your own. This isn't necessarily bad if you have visions that align; in that case, you might become a power duo or a team that creates the vision together! How fun would that be?

Please note that sometimes your fear, insecurity, impatience, and self-doubt can get in the way. This is normal. When moments like this happen, take a step back and ask yourself, "What happens if I don't follow through with the actions to create my vision? What happened to my intention? What happened to the goal I set for myself?" These questions will remind you of your why and why you created your vision in the first place.

With your vision, you have a compass that guides your decisions and helps you lead with confidence, drive, passion, love, and purpose.

This journey begins with you—and your vision will be the guide that lights your way. Once you discover your vision, the journey becomes clearer and way more exciting. Are you ready to discover the leader in you that activates your vision? Let's go!

How to Make the Most of This Book and Workbook

This book contains tips, real-life examples, and fun activities to support you become an excellent leader. Each chapter and section focus on a specific skill, and the workbook exercises will guide you to implement, practice, and master them. Dive in and start your leadership adventure!

CHAPTER 1

WHAT MAKES A LEADER?

What Is Leadership Anyway?
By Lisa Lermitte

Leadership is your ability to turn a vision into reality and how you guide and influence others to achieve that common goal with you. It is a way for you to bring your gifts, talents, and visions and create the impact you were meant to give to the world. It is shown in how you think, act, and feel. There are various personalities of leaders that bring their unique traits and benefits to leading others. You will find you have a natural tendency toward a style. Let's explore yours.

Different Operating Styles of Leadership: Which One Are You?

Everyone has a style of leadership that feels more natural than others. To be an effective leader, knowing your style and understanding the other operating styles in leadership is helpful so you can flex to work with or inspire anyone. Style is like your personality or the way you tend to do things. People with different styles or personalities will receive your style differently. So, learning about all the styles will help you know how to best interact with the other styles because you understand them. Let's review the four styles and see which sounds most like you.

The first style is called Supporter. Supporters are known for leading with their hearts. Empathy comes easily to them, and they care about how people feel along the way. They are naturally great listeners; people feel comfortable opening up to them quickly and giving them a nice long hug. These leaders put others before themselves and tend to be humble. Although softer-spoken, they are powerful leaders, bringing connection and empathy to life. This style's flex in working with others is speaking up and delegating versus doing everything themselves.

The next style is called Analyzer. This style leads with their intellect and enjoys the process as much as progress. Their astute attention to detail and accuracy allows people to trust and depend on them. They tend to be organized planners and keep the big picture in mind along with the next step. They use data to make decisions, and you can count on them to do the job well and in excellence. They may take longer to make decisions for this same reason. Nonetheless, this is another powerful leadership style that brings excellence and order to the world. This style's flex in working with others is to have fun and not be so serious all the time.

Next, we have the style called Controller. This style tends to step up and take control before the others. They have an easy time enrolling others into their vision and usually have magnetic personalities that people are attracted to. They can inspire a group into action. They have no problem delegating or asking for support and are good at getting results. Their boldness and confidence make them powerful leaders. This style's flex is to listen to others and have patience to build connections.

Last but certainly not least, we have the Promoter. This style makes life fun and naturally brings people together with their charismatic personalities. They prefer working with people to working alone and are enjoyable to be around. They tend to operate more freely, be spontaneous, and light up the room with their energy. This type of leader reminds us to enjoy the ride along with the results, and they are powerful enrollers in any vision they believe in. This style's flex in working with others is to stay focused and ground themselves in their vision.

Each style has its strengths and advantages. It's essential for you to understand your style as well as others; this will help you work together with other leaders. Lean into your strengths and learn others' strengths to bring them together. No matter your style, it is always a good idea to listen, ask questions for clarity, and ask for what you want and need. Playing with other leadership styles is more than fun; it enables unity and strong teamwork. Remember, you can go so far alone, but together, we are limitless. Become not just a master of your style but flex into the other styles as well to become a master leader.

Kid Superstars: Real-Life Young Leaders
By Joy Vanichkul

Did you know you don't need to be an adult to make a big difference? Some of today's most influential leaders are young people, just like you, who saw a problem and decided to do something about it. Leadership isn't about waiting for permission; it's about having the courage to act, be creative, and work for change. Let's meet five incredible young leaders who didn't just talk about making a difference and having a global impact; they *achieved it*. Their stories will show you that anyone can be a leader, regardless of age. Their actions have inspired and motivated millions of people.

Malala Yousafzai: The Girl Who Fought for Education

«*Let us pick up our books and pens; they are our most powerful weapons.*»

Imagine this: You're excited to go to school, hang out with your friends, and learn cool stuff. But then, one day, you're told, "Sorry, no more school for you because you're a girl." That's what happened to Malala Yousafzai in Pakistan. But did she stay quiet? Nope! Even after a dangerous attack, Malala spoke out because she believed that everyone—boys and girls—deserves to go to school. While she was on her way home from school, they stopped her bus and hurt her badly. However, Malala didn't give up. She was taken to the hospital, recovered, and became even more determined to fight for every child's right to attend school.

She showed incredible courage. At just seventeen, she became the youngest person ever to win the Nobel Peace Prize! Malala's story teaches us that when you stand up for what's right, you can inspire millions of people and achieve results.

Greta Thunberg: The Teen Who's Saving the Planet

«*I have learned you are never too small to make a difference.*»

At only fifteen, Greta Thunberg began a one-person protest outside the Swedish Parliament, holding a sign that read, "School Strike for Climate." She was frustrated that world leaders weren't doing enough to combat climate change. What started with one girl grew into a global movement called Fridays for Future, where millions of young people joined Greta in demanding action to save the planet.

Greta didn't let her age or size stop her. She believed her actions could inspire others even as one teenager standing alone. She knew that being young or feeling small doesn't mean you can't create change. Every voice matters. Greta's story shows that people will listen when you stand up for something important.

Her boldness and relentless focus on the environment have made her a leading voice for climate action. Greta's story teaches us that no matter how young or small you feel, your voice can have a powerful impact on the world.

Gitanjali Rao: The Inventor for a Better Future

«*I don't look like your typical scientist. Everything I do, I want to make sure it helps others.*»

When Gitanjali Rao learned about the water crisis in Flint, Michigan, she didn't just feel bad; she took action. At only eleven, she invented a device that detects lead in water, which helps protect people from dangerous contamination. However, Gitanjali didn't stop there. She also developed technology to fight cyberbullying and tackle other social issues.

Her creativity and problem-solving skills earned her the title of *TIME* magazine's first-ever Kid of the Year in 2020. Gitanjali's leadership shows that curiosity and innovation can lead to solutions that make a real difference.

Joshua Williams: Feeding People in Need

«*One small act of kindness can lead to a world of change.*»

Ever wonder how one small act of kindness can grow into something *huge*? Just ask Joshua Williams. Joshua gave $20 to a homeless man when he was only four years old, and that simple act sparked something big. By age five, he had started Joshua's Heart Foundation, an organization that helps feed people who don't have enough food. Today, his foundation has provided food to thousands of families. Joshua shows us that you don't have to wait to be a grown-up to help others; sometimes, all it takes is a kind heart and the willingness to make a difference. Leadership can be as simple as caring for the people around you, and Joshua's kindness got actual results.

Emma González: Speaking Up for Safety

«*Fight for your lives before it's someone else's job.*»

Emma González was a high school senior when tragedy struck her school in Parkland, Florida. After surviving a school shooting, Emma became one of the loudest voices calling for gun safety reform. She co-founded March for Our Lives, a youth-led movement that demands safer schools and communities. Emma's heartfelt speeches and emotional resilience have inspired young people everywhere to get involved and take action. Her leadership shows that when something isn't right, you don't have to wait for someone else to fix it. You can stand up, speak out, and be the change you want to see.

You Can Be a Leader, Too.

What's the secret to becoming a leader like Malala, Greta, Gitanjali, Joshua, or Emma? It's simple: Believe in something, take action, and achieve results. These young leaders didn't wait for someone else to solve the problem; they acted, stayed determined, and made a real difference.

What about you? What's something you care about that you want to change? It could be environmental protection, helping others, or making your school a better place. Leadership isn't about being the loudest or the oldest; it's about being true to yourself and positively impacting the world around you. Stay true to yourself, and you'll find the confidence and self-assurance to lead.

Remember, you're never too young to start making a difference. It all begins with a tiny step. The world needs leaders like *you*, so take that step, use your voice, and make things happen!

CHAPTER 2

BUILD YOUR SUPERPOWER

Belief in Yourself Is Key
By Sarit Atwood

Okay, superstar! Now that you understand what makes a leader, we'll discuss something super important: confidence.

Confidence is that awesome feeling when you believe in yourself, like when you're about to sing your favorite song, try out for a sports team, or make a new friend. Having confidence is like having your very own superpower.

Let me tell you a brief story about me and a story about Benny. I wanted to sing in front of my sixth-grade class when I was around your age, but I was super nervous. I worried, *What if I mess up?* Or *What if my classmates laugh at me?* But then, I remembered my mom had told me a secret earlier in life: "Confidence isn't about being perfect. It's about believing in yourself even when things are a little scary."

I decided to give it a try. I stood before my class with my hands shaking, took a deep breath, and started singing. And guess what? Some kids smiled, some clapped, and even though I made a tiny mistake, I felt *amazing*! I realized it wasn't about being perfect; it was about being brave enough to try. That's when I discovered that confidence grows every time we face our fears.

Finding Your Voice: Benny's Journey to Confidence

Benny was the type of teen who had a lot going for him: He was smart, funny, and had great friends. However, there was one thing that always made him feel anxious: speaking up in class. All the other kids made it look easy, but every time Benny tried, his voice would catch in his throat, and he'd freeze.

One afternoon, his best friend, Lucy, noticed him sitting quietly during a group discussion. "Hey, Benny," she said, "You got this. The only thing in your way is you. You just need to believe in yourself and take it step by step."

Benny wasn't sure he believed her, but something about the way she said it made him think. He knew he couldn't avoid speaking up forever. So, with Lucy giving him an encouraging nod, he took a deep breath, swallowed his nerves, and decided to raise his hand. He started to speak—but he stumbled over his words.

Benny felt embarrassed. He had thought this time would be different. However, Lucy wasn't about to let him give up. "Benny, that was great! You tried! Now, let's do it again—don't overthink it."

Even though he still wasn't confident, Benny tried again—and again. With each attempt, he found his voice a little more. Something clicked in his mind on his fifth try, and he finally spoke without hesitation. He couldn't believe it! Some of his classmates even gave him a thumbs-up, but what felt even better was that he proved to himself that he could do it.

Benny realized that building confidence is a lot like practicing for anything, whether it's speaking up, sports, or school. It's not about being perfect the first time. It's about showing up and pushing through even when scared or uncertain. By taking one step at a time and not giving up, Benny finally believed in himself. Now, it's your turn to grow your confidence!

CONFIDENCE WORKBOOK

Let's do a fun challenge together.

Step 1: Identify what's holding you back.

Think about something you feel nervous or unsure about. It could be reading aloud in class, trying a new sport, or even asking someone to be your friend or play with you. Once you've identified one thing that is holding you back, write it down or draw a picture of it.

Exercise: Take a moment to reflect: What do you need to believe in yourself and to take the first step? Write your thoughts below:

_____
_____
_____

Step 2: Take a small step forward.

Next, decide on a tiny step to face that fear, just like Benny did. Maybe it's practicing in front of a mirror, asking a friend to join you, or telling a grown-up how you feel.

Exercise: The small step I'm committed to taking is

_____
_____
_____

Step 3: Cheer yourself on!

Every time you try something new, even if it's not perfect, say something positive to yourself, like "I'm proud of myself for trying" or "I'm getting better every time."

Exercise: The "believe in me" cheer I'm choosing from the examples above is:
_____
_____
_____

You got this, superstar! Remember, confidence is all about trying, learning, and believing in yourself no matter what. Keep shining bright, and never be afraid to take that next step!

Talk Yourself Up: Positive Self-Talk and Affirmations
By Dr. Joan Yue

Hey there! Are you ready to become your biggest cheerleader? We're diving into the power of positive self-talk and daily affirmations. You'll learn how to boost your self-esteem, believe in your abilities, and pave the way to become an awesome leader.

Why Positive Self-Talk Matters

Think about how you talk to yourself when you make a mistake or face a challenge. Do you get down on yourself or encourage yourself to try again? How you speak to yourself greatly affects how you feel and act.

Positive self-talk is about speaking to yourself in a kind and encouraging way. It's like having a supportive friend inside your head. Instead of saying, "I can't do this," you might say, "I'll give it my best shot." This slight shift in language can change your mindset and increase your confidence.

How Daily Affirmations Work

Affirmations are positive sentences you say repeatedly to feel confident and stop negative thoughts.

For example, saying, "I am a strong leader," helps you believe in your leadership skills more.

Here's why affirmations are so cool:

- **They program your brain:** Repeating positive statements helps your brain start to believe them. It's like training your brain to think in a new, positive way.

- **They boost motivation:** On days when you're not feeling 100 percent, affirmations remind you what you can achieve.
- **They help you feel more relaxed:** Focusing on positive thoughts can help reduce stress and make challenges more manageable.

Creating Your Affirmation Routine

Starting your affirmation routine is easy and fun.
Here's how you can do it:

1. **Pick your affirmations:** Choose a few positive statements that mean something to you. They should be short, clear, and in the present tense, like, "I am capable and strong" or "I am a courageous and inspiring leader."
You can even make them fun, like, "It's so ridiculous how naturally leadership comes to me," or "It's crazy how much people love my speeches!"

2. **Say them daily:** Repeat your affirmations out loud every morning and write them on paper two to three times daily. You can even make a poster to hang in your room.

3. **Believe in them:** Believing in what you're saying is important. Imagine how it feels to be the person in your affirmations.

You can also make them more engaging with a variety of fun activities.

- **Mirror talk:** Stand in front of a mirror each morning, look yourself in the eyes, and say your affirmations out loud. This helps you connect with yourself and start the day positively.
- **Affirmation jar:** Write different affirmations on slips of paper and put them in a jar. Each day, pull one out and focus on it.
- **Affirmation buddy:** Pair up with a friend and exchange affirmations. Hearing someone else say something positive about you can make it easier to believe.

Overcoming the Challenges

Using positive self-talk and affirmations can sometimes feel weird, especially if you often think badly about yourself. Here's how to stick with it:

- **Be patient:** Change doesn't happen overnight. It takes time to shift your thoughts.

- **Keep it real:** Your affirmations should be believable. They might feel unrealistic if they're too far from where you currently are. For example, if you want to cultivate trust in people, starting with the affirmation, "I trust everyone," might feel like too big a step. To ease into the feeling of trust, begin with something smaller, like, "I trust my dog." Gradually, you can build up to "I trust my Mom" and "I trust my friends." Over time, as your comfort grows, you can work your way up to saying, "I trust everyone."
- **Mix it up:** Change your affirmations to match your growing confidence and new goals.

Why This Matters

By learning to talk positively to yourself and using affirmations, you're not just improving your self-esteem but setting the foundation for solid leadership. Leaders need to believe in themselves to inspire and lead others effectively.

Ready to start talking yourself up? Remember, every leader began somewhere and probably used a lot of positive self-talk along the way. Now, it's your turn to boost yourself up and discover the leader in you.

Keep these tools in your back pocket, use them daily, and watch how they transform your thinking about yourself and your leadership abilities. You've got this!

How to Courageously Tackle Fears and Smash Insecurities
By Valery B Ireland

Let's be real: Everyone feels fear and insecurity sometimes. It's just part of being human. However, the difference between someone who's courageous and someone who's not is how they deal with it. Courage isn't about being fearless. It's about showing up, taking action, and moving forward despite the fear. No matter how confident they seem, every leader has had moments where fear creeps in. But here's the secret: They don't let it stop them. Instead, they courageously push through it and stay committed to their vision. This is how you grow into the leader you're meant to be.

Think of a time when you were scared to do something, but you did it anyway. How did you feel afterward? That's courage. Every time you take a step forward, even when it's uncomfortable, you build your courage muscle and strengthen your mind and heart.

The Truth About Fear

Fear often shows up bigger than it really is. It convinces you that bad things will happen even when there's no proof. Have you ever felt afraid of something only to realize it wasn't as scary as you thought? That's because fear often stands for:

False
Evidence
Appearing
Real

And that is exactly how it works. Fear thrives on uncertainty and exaggerates adverse outcomes. It convinces us that worst-case scenarios are reality even when they're not. However, you don't have to let fear control your actions.

Instead, choose to:

Face
Everything
And
Rise

This is the courageous response to fear. Instead of letting it paralyze you, confront it, take action, and grow from the experience. Every time you tackle a fear, you strengthen your courage muscle. This is your innate power. Allow me to explain why.

The word "courage" comes from the Latin word "cor," meaning "heart." At its core, courage is about having the heart to keep going even when it's tough. It's not about being fearless but about acting with heart and bravery even when fear exists. God has given you a spirit not of fear but of power, love, and self-control. Courage is your superpower! It allows you to break through insecurities, face life's challenges, and become the leader you're meant to be. The more you use it, the more unstoppable you'll feel. Whether it's trying something new, standing up for yourself, or chasing your dreams, courage is the key to it all.

This is what courage can look like:

Standing tall when it feels easier to sit down.

Speaking up when it feels easier to stay silent.

Pursuing your dreams even when doubt tries to hold you back.

True leaders are committed to their goals and dreams. They don't just talk about it; they take action. Being courageous requires commitment. Commitment is about being intentional and choosing to do what it takes, even when the path gets tough. When you have a vision for your life, sometimes, you get to make bold moves, be different, and risk failing. However, it's through those moments you get stronger. Taking risks, getting creative in tough situations, and showing up as your true self make you courageous. You might face criticism or even failure, but that's when courage really kicks in. It's the decision to get up, face your fears head-on, and use them as motivation to build resilience and inner strength.

The Courage-Building Formula: Keys to Strengthening Your Courage Muscle

Building courage is a process that develops over time and requires intentional effort. Here are powerful strategies to help you strengthen your courage and lead with confidence:

- **Intentionality:** Focus on what truly matters. When your priorities are clear, it becomes easier to make courageous decisions. Are you willing to say no to distractions and yes to what fuels your growth?

- **Purpose:** A strong why drives courage. Understanding the deeper reason behind your actions helps you push through fear. What's your why for taking bold steps?

- **Curiosity:** Stay open to new experiences. Growth happens when you're willing to explore the unknown and see challenges as learning opportunities. What can you discover from this challenge?

- **Commitment:** Dedicate yourself to your goals even when the path is difficult. Courage means sticking with your vision no matter how hard it gets. Are you willing to persevere through tough times?

- **Risk-Taking:** Courage grows with every small, calculated risk you take. Failure is part of the journey, and every misstep teaches valuable lessons. What small risk can you take today to strengthen your courage?

- **Adaptability:** Life is unpredictable, and courage involves being flexible when things don't go as planned. How can you adjust your approach and keep moving forward when challenges arise?

- **Acceptance:** Embrace difficulties as opportunities for growth instead of obstacles. Let go of rigid expectations and embrace the possibilities. Can you welcome change and see it as a stepping stone to success?

- **Creativity:** When faced with challenges, think outside the box. Creative problem-solving can turn tough situations into opportunities for growth. How can you approach this challenge with a fresh perspective?

By practicing these strategies, you'll notice your courage muscle strengthening, allowing you to lead with confidence, embrace challenges, and grow through every experience.

The more you practice courage, the more natural it becomes. Soon, you'll start to see that fear isn't a wall blocking your way; it's an opportunity to level up.

Ask yourself: What's one fear you can face today? What insecurity are you ready to smash? The only thing standing between you and your next level of leadership is one decision: to take action despite the fear.

You were born to be courageous. It's already inside of you. Just take the first step, and you'll see how strong you really are. Go ahead—face your fears, smash those insecurities, and lead like the bold, unstoppable leader you're becoming!

COURAGE WORKBOOK

This workbook is designed to help you build the courage to be your most confident, bold self every day. Through practical exercises and self-reflection, you will uncover your strengths, celebrate your wins, and discover new ways to handle challenges with courage and resilience.

Remember that courage is like a muscle—the more you work on it, the stronger it becomes.

Exercise 1: Crafting Daily Declarations

To build your courage, speaking words of empowerment over yourself is important. Begin each day by writing down positive declarations. These statements will remind you of your inner strength and resilience.

Here are some declaration examples:

- **Freedom:** I am free to be myself, unafraid of others' opinions.
- **Self-Belief:** I trust my ability to do great things.
- **Boldness:** I will try new things even if they initially seem difficult and daunting.

Now, it's your turn:

Write three powerful declarations that you will say aloud each morning to help you develop your courage and confidence throughout the day.

1. _____
2. _____
3. _____

Exercise 2: Reflect on Your Courageous Achievements

Think about moments in your life when you acted courageously, whether it was trying something new, standing up for yourself, or facing a fear. Reflect on what you learned from those experiences.

Here is an example:

- **Achievement:** I was nervous about joining the soccer team, but I went for it.
- **Lesson:** I discovered that trying new things is exciting and rewarding, and I made great friends along the way.

Now, it's your turn:

Write down three moments when you were courageous. How did those moments make you feel stronger and more confident or capable?

1. _____
2. _____
3. _____

Exercise 3: Identify Your Strengths

Everyone has unique strengths that shape who they are. These qualities are what help you act courageously. Think about the personal strengths that you use to face challenges in your daily life.

Here are some examples of strengths:

- **Resilience:** I bounce back after difficulties and keep moving forward.
- **Leadership:** I set an example for others by standing strong in my values.
- **Kindness:** I show kindness even when it's difficult because it takes courage to be compassionate.

Now, it's your turn:

Write five of your strengths and reflect on how they help you act courageously in different situations.

1. _____
   _____

2. _____
   _____

3. _____
   _____

4. _____
   _____

5. _____
   _____

Exercise 4: Courage Challenges

Now that you've reflected on your past, it's time to set new challenges to continue growing your courage. Facing your fears head-on is a powerful way to strengthen your courage muscle.

Reflection Questions

- What is something courageous you did today?

_____
_____
_____

- What small challenge can you face tomorrow that will require courage?

_____
_____
_____

- How can you reframe something that scares you into an opportunity for growth?

_____
_____
_____

Exercise 5: Courageous Declarations for Strength

Use the following declarations as inspiration to create your own. Each one reminds you of how capable you are in moments that require courage.

1. I am excited to try new things and embrace challenges.
2. I trust in my ability to handle whatever comes my way with grace.
3. I stand up for what is right, even when it's difficult.

Now, it's your turn:

Create three new declarations that will help you build your courage daily.

1. _____
   _____
2. _____
   _____
3. _____
   _____

Exercise 6: Strengthening Through Action

Courage is not just a feeling; it's a practice. Write actions you can take in the next week that will strengthen your courage muscle:

- What fear can you face this week, and how will you approach it?

_____
_____
_____

- What small step can you take toward a bigger goal that will require courage?

_____
_____
_____

- Who can you support or stand up for that would benefit from your courageous leadership?

_____
_____
_____

Next Steps in Your Courage Journey

- **Practice:** Continue practicing being courageous by trying new things, speaking up, and pushing past your comfort zone.
- **Look for opportunities:** Seek moments to be courageous, whether it's standing up for yourself or others, taking on a new challenge, or showing kindness when it's difficult.
- **Embrace the fear:** Courage isn't the absence of fear; it's acting despite it. Every time you move through fear, you become stronger.

You are courageous, resilient, and capable. Every time you take a bold step, you strengthen your confidence and build the foundation for future success.

This workbook is your guide to keep moving forward, reflect on your courage, and rise to new challenges. Embrace every part of the journey. You've got this!

CHAPTER 3

COMMUNICATION IS COOL

Listen Up! How to Be an Awesome Listener
By Melissa Windell

Listen! Who needs to listen anyway, right?

Teachers are always talking; parents are constantly telling us what to do.

It is *sooooo* boring and annoying.

I feel you in that. I highly dislike being told what to do, and I also didn't enjoy listening to other people all that much until I heard this great phrase.

"We have two ears and one mouth so that we can listen twice as much as we talk."
—*Epictetus, a Greek Philosopher*

What do you think when you read that?

I heard that we humans are meant to hear, listen, be present more than we are meant to talk. For there is great knowledge and wisdom when we listen to other people speak.

Don't get me wrong; your voice matters, and we want you to use your voice.

Your voice, heart, vision for your dreams, and life matter. Your voice has meaning. Your voice shares the gift of who you are out into the world, and trust me when I say this: The world wants to hear your voice and what you have to share.

As you get older, you will learn that there is a time and place for everything. You will begin to know when it is a great time to speak up and when it is a great time to listen.

Speaking with thought, intention, and mindfulness is an art all its own, but that is a topic for a different day.

Right now, we will talk about listening, an entirely different skill set.

There are four main styles of listening. On the next page, you will see the four main styles; I will describe each one in detail shortly.

1. Listening
2. Deep Listening
3. Listening to what's underneath the listening
4. Listening to your intuition

1. Listening

When you listen to other people talk, it lets them know you care about them. It is not just about you. You want to hear what they say.

It delivers a message to them that:

- They matter.
- They are seen.
- They are heard.
- They are valued as persons.

Healthy listening involves taking turns. First, let them speak for a few minutes while you listen. Then, respond by sharing something related to what they said, and they reply to your response. For example: Brody is telling his buddy Joey a story about the soccer game he just had. Joey might reply something like: "Wow, that seems like a great game! How did it feel to play that position?" Once Brody responds, he also can ask Joey what cool thing happened in his day.

Next, switch.

This is called taking turns talking, just like you take turns playing sports, swinging on the swings, or when you are messaging with a friend.

When we listen to people, we:

- Build relationships and friendships
- Create connections with them
- Support each other
- Do better in school, sports, and careers

This creates an atmosphere that offers opportunities for lasting relationships to be built and for opportunities like games, experiences, and projects to be created with a feeling of ease, good communication, and fun, creating better results.

It allows you and the other person to see each other's points of view and find a balance that leaves you both feeling good, creating a happy relationship and team-building experience.

2. Deep Listening

Deep listening is one of the biggest gifts you can give anyone—truly. It is listening without just listening so you can talk. It is listening without interrupting and without interjecting your thoughts and opinions.

Deep listening is holding space for someone to share their raw, vulnerable, truest emotions without judgment or thoughts—just listening.

Have you ever had a hard moment in life, cried (or wanted to cry), and just wanted to be heard—nothing else? You wanted someone to just listen to you spill all your emotions, thoughts, and feelings and let you be as messy and vulnerable as you want or need to be.

And they just listen. Maybe they will give you a hug or a tissue; however, they mostly quietly listen with their presence, heart, and compassion. You know they care just by them being there.

If you have felt this from someone, I trust you know how incredible it feels. And if you haven't, I will tell you from firsthand experience that it is the biggest gift anyone has ever given me.

It is also the biggest gift I have been able to give to anyone else.

Try it. See what happens.

Also, don't be shy about asking someone to do it for you. It could sound like this, "Hey, I have a lot going through my mind and heart right now, and I could use someone just to listen to me. Do not give me any advice or opinions; just listen to me. Would you mind doing that for me?"

Most people will be grateful to let you share what's on your mind and heart.

3. Listening to What's Underneath the Listening

What does that even mean, right? Let me explain.

You know when a friend or parent is "hangry." They are being rude, mean, and short with you, but what is underneath it is that they are hungry.

Another example is when you are in P.E. class, and the teacher makes you pick teams. Someone gets angry or upset about being picked last or the team they are on and throws a tantrum. What could be underneath it is that they feel rejected, not good enough, and embarrassed.

Listening from the emotional part of yourself, your intuition, and your senses (like *I get a sense that they are actually feeling sad, not mad*) allows you to help them move through their emotions and better understand themselves.

The one thing to be aware of and careful with is to not come from a place of assuming you know what it is or projecting your thoughts onto them.

Listening with curiosity and asking them questions with curiosity will be your best friend in these moments.

It lets them know you're asking them from a place of love and compassion, not judgment.

Ask them questions like:

- I can see you are upset. Are you okay?
- Is there something else you need?
- What are you feeling right now?
- It seems like you are angry about _____. I am curious. If you feel like sharing, what are you really angry or upset about? What's really bothering you?

When listening to what's underneath the listening, you are better at understanding someone and helping them better understand themselves so they can heal and feel better and lighter.

4. Listening to Your Intuition

This is my personal favorite.

We are all born with this magnificent thing called intuition. It can sound like a soft, whisper-like voice, a strong feeling in your stomach, or a knowingness—you just know but can't explain why. It also can come in dreams or be something you feel in your body when someone talks (think goosebumps/chills).

These are all signs of your intuition speaking to you. Your intuition is your secret built-in navigation to walk through life. We all have it.

It is your higher self.

Our higher self is the wise being within all of us. It is a calm, loving, and spiritual guide that supports us in life.

It can see what is going on behind the scenes.

It is your ability to understand something immediately.

Your higher self is your intuition speaking to you constantly.

For example, have you ever walked into a room and the hair on the back of your neck stood up?

Or have you walked into a room, and it felt scary or creepy?

Or maybe you met someone for the first time and knew right away, you would get along with that person.

Or someone said something to you, and you knew they were not being fully honest. You had no proof you just had that "feeling."

These are all examples of your intuition talking, and the more you listen to it, the stronger it gets and the further it will take you in life. It is your higher self. It is God giving you insight about what to go after and what to steer clear of because your intuition can see things you can't.

It is your built-in navigation system.

Your intuition also can give you images, thoughts, or a sense of knowingness when it comes to your visions.

You are probably already using your intuition in many ways, and it comes in unique ways for all of us.

I will share a few personal examples:

My daughter and I had been thinking about adopting an older dog. One morning, we got up to go on a hike, and on the way to the hike, I got a mental download to go to the humane society instead. So, we did. When we arrived, a puppy was outside playing, and I knew in my body that she would be our puppy. Two weeks later, we took her home. She turned out to be the perfect dog and matched all our desires in a dog (minus the older dog part).

Another example is when I had the most vivid dream when I was in high school. I am not a dreamer, and this dream had four people—in detail—I had never seen before. We were in a restaurant-style kitchen.

I shrugged the dream off but knew it felt real. Three years later, I moved to a different state and got a job at a sandwich shop. One day, while at work, the exact memory of my dream came to real life. Some people call this deja vu—the exact same people and environment.

I told the people I was working with—who I had a dream about years earlier—about the dream. One of them said to me, "It means you are in the right place at the right time." That always stuck with me.

Your intuition may show up this way, too, leading you toward a vision, feelings, or realities that others can't quite see yet or explain.

Follow it. Believe in it. Trust your intuition that you can *do it* and that you are exactly who you need to be to follow through with it.

The visions might come when you're young or later in life. They might change over time or be added to. It is all perfect. It is all meant to be.

Spirit—your higher self, your intuition—is always guiding you. Listening to it is your choice.

Talk the Talk: Speak Clearly and Confidently
By Shavonne Cook

Imagine you're sitting in class, and the teacher asks a question you know the answer to. Your heart starts pounding, your palms get sweaty, and you feel like all eyes are on you. Instead of raising your hand, you stay quiet, hoping someone else will speak up. Does this sound familiar? If so, you're not alone. Many teens experience moments of shyness and fear when it comes to speaking up. However, here's the good news: Speaking clearly and confidently is a skill you can learn and improve with practice. This section will explore overcoming shyness and speaking up with clarity and confidence.

Understanding Shyness

Shyness is a feeling of apprehension or discomfort in social situations, especially when speaking in front of others. It's normal to feel this way, and even adults experience shyness. The key to overcoming shyness is to understand where it comes from. Often, it's a fear of judgment, making a mistake, or feeling like you have nothing valuable to say.

Everyone has felt nervous or shy at some point, even the most confident people you see around you. What sets them apart is that they've learned how to manage their shyness. Instead of letting it hold them back, they use it as a signal to prepare and practice.

The Importance of Speaking Up

Speaking up isn't just about being heard; it's about sharing your ideas, asking questions, and contributing to conversations. When you speak up, you show that you're engaged and interested. It's a way to build connections with others, express your thoughts, and influence the world around you. Whether it's in class, during a group project, or in everyday conversations, having the confidence to speak up can make a big difference in how people see you and how you see yourself.

Strategies to Overcome Shyness

1. **Start small:** Begin by speaking up in situations where you feel most comfortable. It could be with close friends, family, or in a small group. The more you practice speaking up in low-pressure situations, the easier it will become in larger groups.

2. **Prepare and practice:** Preparation is the key to confidence. If you know you have to speak in front of a group, practice what you want to say. Rehearse in

front of a mirror, record yourself, or ask a friend to listen. The more familiar you are with your material, the less nervous you will feel, and the more natural the speech will be.

3. **Focus on your message—not yourself:** It's easy to become self-conscious when you're nervous. Instead of worrying about how you look or sound, focus on the message you want to convey. Think about why it's important and how it could help others.

4. **Use positive self-talk:** Your mind can be your biggest supporter or your worst enemy. Instead of telling yourself, "I'm too shy to speak up," try saying, "I have something valuable to contribute." Positive affirmations can help shift your mindset from one of fear to one of confidence.

5. **Embrace mistakes:** No one is perfect, and everyone makes mistakes. Don't be afraid to stumble over a word or forget what you are going to say. Instead of seeing mistakes as failures, view them as opportunities to learn and grow. Remember, every great speaker started somewhere.

6. **Practice active listening:** Good communication isn't just about speaking; it's also about listening. When you actively listen to others, you can respond more thoughtfully, which can build your confidence in conversations.

Tips for Speaking Clearly and Confidently

1. **Slow down:** We tend to speak faster when we're nervous. Slow down your speech to ensure your words are clear and easy to understand. This also gives you more time to think about the next words you'll say.

2. **Maintain eye contact:** Eye contact shows confidence and helps you connect with your audience. Start by making eye contact with one person at a time. If looking directly at someone makes you nervous, try looking at the space between their eyebrows. It will still appear as though you're making eye contact.

3. **Use body language:** Your body language can say a lot about your confidence level. Stand or sit up straight, use hand gestures to emphasize your points, and avoid fidgeting. Confident body language can also help you feel more confident mentally.

4. **Breathe deeply:** Deep breathing helps calm your nerves and provides the oxygen your brain needs to function clearly. Before speaking, take a deep breath in, hold it for a few seconds, and exhale slowly. This simple exercise can help you feel more grounded and focused.

5. **Practice pausing:** Don't be afraid to pause during your speech. Pauses can be powerful; they give you a moment to collect your thoughts and give your audience a moment to absorb what you've said.

6. **Seek feedback:** After speaking, ask for feedback from someone you trust. Constructive criticism can help you improve your speaking skills over time. Remember, feedback is not a reflection of your worth but an opportunity for growth.

Exercises to Build Confidence

1. **The mirror exercise:** Practice speaking in front of a mirror for a few minutes each day. Focus on your facial expressions, eye contact, and body language. This exercise helps you become more aware of how you appear when you speak.

2. **The thirty-second speech:** Choose a random topic and speak about it for thirty seconds without stopping. This exercise helps you think on your feet and practice speaking clearly without preparation.

3. **Storytelling practice:** Share a story with a friend or family member. Pay attention to how you engage your listener and use your voice to convey emotions and emphasis.

4. **Join a club or group:** Consider joining a club like debate, drama, or a public speaking group. These clubs provide a supportive environment for practicing speaking and receiving feedback from others.

Speaking with clarity and confidence is a journey, not a destination. It's a skill that takes time, practice, and patience to develop. Remember, everyone feels nervous at times, and that's okay. The important thing is to keep pushing yourself out of your comfort zone and to celebrate your progress along the way. By learning to "Talk the Talk," you're not just finding your voice but discovering your power to lead and make a difference. So go ahead, speak up, and let the world hear what you have to say.

SPEAKING UP WORKBOOK

Questions to understand you better:

1. What situations make you feel most nervous about speaking up, and why?

_____
_____
_____

2. What is one thing you can do this week to practice speaking more confidently?

_____
_____
_____

3. How can you use the tips and exercises from this chapter to help someone else who might be struggling with shyness?

_____
_____
_____

By embracing and practicing these techniques, you'll be well on your way to becoming a confident speaker and leader. Remember, your voice matters, you matter, and what you have to say matters!

Say It Without Words: The Power of Non-Verbal Communication
By Jeroselle "Jiji" Chai, BSN-RN

Picture this: You're in the middle of a team challenge and have to lead your group without saying a word. It might feel impossible, but there's a way to get your message across. You use your body, expressions, and energy. That's non-verbal communication—an essential skill for any leader.

Non-verbal communication is the ability to express thoughts and emotions through body language, facial expressions, and eye contact. As a leader, your presence often speaks louder than your words. This unspoken language can shape how others perceive you, and learning to master it helps you build stronger connections and influence those around you.

This non-verbal communication is shown in your body language. As a teen becoming a leader, how you carry yourself is crucial. Here are some tips to understand your body language:

- **Posture:** Standing tall shows confidence. It says you're ready to handle challenges. Slouching, on the other hand, might give off the impression of insecurity or disengagement. Stand like you mean what you say.
- **Gestures:** Movements like a firm handshake or a confident thumbs-up can show others you believe in yourself. Avoid overusing nervous habits like fidgeting, which can show uncertainty.
- **Movement:** Walking with purpose shows determination. Moving lazily or dragging your feet might communicate boredom or lack of interest.

Reading Facial Expressions

Your face tells a story without you ever saying a word. Learning to read and use facial expressions can significantly impact how others respond to you.

- **Smiling:** A genuine smile can break down barriers and create trust. It invites others in and shows openness.
- **Frowning:** When you frown or look tense, people may interpret it as frustration or dissatisfaction. As a leader, managing your emotions when speaking or leading is important.
- **Eye Contact:** Good eye contact shows you're listening and engaged. Avoiding eye contact might make you seem distracted or insecure.

As you grow into leadership, mastering non-verbal communication will set you apart. Whether you're leading a group project, giving a class presentation, or simply making new friends, people pay attention to how you carry yourself. Understanding non-verbal cues can elevate your influence and help you express leadership in every interaction.

The New Kid on the Block

Let's meet Jenny, a high school sophomore starting fresh at a new school. Jenny was used to her old friends, and stepping into a new environment felt like a major challenge. She didn't know anyone, and with each step down the hallway, it felt like everyone already had their groups and cliques.

On her first day, Jenny found herself sitting alone at lunch, trying to look busy with her phone. She scanned the cafeteria, hoping someone would notice her, but no one did. She slouched over, fiddling with her hair and avoiding eye contact. Her body language screamed, "I'm uncomfortable!"

That's when someone approached her. Sarah, a confident junior with an easy smile, came over. "Hey, you're new here, right? Want to join us?" Jenny was hesitant but felt slightly more at ease because Sarah's body language was warm. She stood tall, smiled, and leaned in slightly, showing Jenny she was genuinely interested.

Sarah made Jenny feel welcome without a single word, using non-verbal cues that showed inclusion. Jenny learned an important leadership lesson that day: Sometimes, how you say something is more important than what you say.

Over the next few weeks, Jenny learned to pay attention to non-verbal communication in herself and others. She noticed how people used gestures, like high-fives after a successful group discussion or how a pat on the back made someone feel supported after a tough day.

In her leadership class, Jenny was part of a project that required the group to work as a team. She watched how her teammates communicated non-verbally. The confident ones made solid eye contact and gestured clearly when sharing their ideas, while others who were more nervous fidgeted or avoided direct eye contact. Jenny realized that understanding these cues made her a better teammate and future leader.

One day, Jenny noticed another new student sitting alone, just like she had been. Remembering how Sarah's body language had made her feel seen, Jenny decided to pass it on. She walked over with a confident posture, smiled warmly, and invited the new student to join her table.

That small act of non-verbal communication broke the ice, and soon enough, they were laughing and sharing stories. Jenny learned firsthand that leadership isn't just about leading big projects; it's about making others feel comfortable and valued, even in everyday situations.

Jenny's final test of non-verbal communication came when it was time for a big class presentation. Normally, Jenny would feel nervous speaking in front of others, but this time, she used her non-verbal skills to her advantage. She stood tall, projected confidence, and used her hands to illustrate her points. She maintained good eye contact with the audience, engaging them with a smile every now and then.

By the end of the presentation, Jenny's classmates were fully engaged, clapping and giving positive feedback. Jenny learned that showing confidence in her non-verbal communication could elevate her leadership skills, helping her make a lasting impression without saying a word.

The Leadership Takeaway

Whether you're navigating new friendships, leading a group, or stepping up to give a presentation, your body language and expressions play a key role in how others perceive you. True leaders pay attention to how they come across and use non-verbal communication to inspire trust, build relationships, and communicate strength—even without words.

COMMUNICATION WORKBOOK

Exercise 1: Active Listening Challenge

Objective: Improve your listening skills by focusing fully on others. Leaders listen more than they speak, absorbing important details before responding.

1. **Pair up:** Grab a friend or family member and have them talk about their day or an event.
2. **Listen up:** Focus entirely on what they're saying—no distractions, no interruptions.
3. **Reflect back:** After they finish, summarize their story back to them. See how much you caught and ask how well you understood.
4. **Takeaway:** Write one thing you learned from this exercise that will make you a better listener.

_____
_____
_____

Exercise 2: Say It Without Words—The Silent Communication Game

Objective: Practice leading and communicating with others using only non-verbal cues, such as facial expressions, gestures, and body language.

1. **Partner up:** Get a friend or family member to join you in this activity.
2. **Pick a situation:** Choose one of these scenarios to act out using only non-verbal communication:
   - You're late for an important event.
   - You need help with a difficult task.
   - You're excited about great news.
   - You're frustrated with something that's not working.
3. **No talking:** Act out the scenario using gestures, facial expressions, and body language. Try to communicate your feelings and needs without speaking.

4. **Guess and feedback:** After you act it out, have your partner guess what you're trying to communicate. Then, switch roles.

5. **Reflect:** Write what was easy or hard about communicating non-verbally. How can mastering non-verbal cues help you as a leader?

_____
_____
_____

Exercise 3: Non-Verbal Communication Detective

Objective: Learn to read non-verbal cues—an essential skill for understanding emotions and leading with empathy.

1. **Watch a TV show or movie:** Pick a show with lots of conversations or interactions.

2. **Observe closely:** Watch how characters use body language and facial expressions. What can you tell about their feelings without hearing the words?

3. **Capture it:** Either draw or cut out pictures of different emotional expressions you see (happiness, surprise, worry, confidence).

4. **Interpret:** Write the emotions you notice and how the characters express them without speaking. How could you use similar body language to lead confidently and show empathy?

Reflection Questions

Write three key things you learned about yourself through these exercises. How can improving your non-verbal communication skills help you be a better leader?

1. _____
   _____

2. _____
   _____

3. _____
   _____

CHAPTER 4

SOLVE IT LIKE A PRO

How to Solve Problems Like a Boss
By Mack Kyles

Let's face it—problems are everywhere. However, instead of seeing them as roadblocks, leaders see problems as opportunities for growth.

As a leader, the person in charge, you will have problems to solve. And the people you support will look to you for direction. Don't fret. I want to share with you what I learned from my twenty years in the military as a combat Veteran and now as a business owner.

First, there is always a solution.

As leaders, we see problems, roadblocks, and issues as opportunities. If you want to tackle challenges like a leader, here's a step-by-step way to handle anything life throws you.

1. Clearly identify what the real problem is.

Why it matters: You can't fix something if you don't know what's broken, right? Getting clear on the actual problem will keep you from spending time and energy on an issue that does not fix the problem.

Example: Say you're falling behind in school because you've packed your schedule with too many extracurriculars. If you just think, *Everything's too much,* you'll feel stuck. However, if you realize the problem is overcommitting, you'll know what to fix.

2. Gather all the info.

Why it matters: You get to know all available details before jumping into action. The more you understand the problem, the better your chances of solving it. Plus, making decisions without enough information can lead to more trouble down the line.

Example: If you're behind in school, start by looking at your schedule, deadlines, and how much time you're spending on each activity. It'll help you get a clear picture of where your time is going and what's realistic.

3. Brainstorm all possible solutions.

Why it matters: When you get creative and think of different solutions, you create more options. Even the wild ideas can spark something useful. Don't limit yourself—just get all the ideas out there.

Example: Your ideas might include cutting back on activities, asking teachers for deadline extensions, or setting up a better study schedule. No judgment yet; just come up with as many solutions as you can.

4. Pick the best option.

Why it matters: Not every solution will work equally well. You need to weigh the pros and cons and figure out what's best for you. Don't stress out about choosing the wrong option because step 6 is available to every leader.

Example: Maybe you brainstormed two ideas: cutting extracurriculars or managing your time better. After thinking it through, you decide better time management makes more sense because you get to keep doing what you love and stay on top of your schoolwork.

5. Make a plan and take action.

Why it matters: A solid plan is what turns your ideas into real results. Without a plan, it's easy to get frustrated or give up. A clear, step-by-step approach helps you stay focused and confident.

Example: Your plan might involve using a planner to block out time for studying, setting personal deadlines, and checking in on your progress every week.

6. Check in and adjust.

Why it matters: Even the best plans need some tweaking. Reflecting on how things went helps you learn from the experience and improve. It's all about growing as you go.

Example: After a week of your new time management system, you realize you still feel stressed on certain days. Reflecting on it shows you might need to focus on prioritizing tasks better. No big deal—just tweak the plan and keep going.

The Leader's Mindset

Problems aren't here to stop you; they're here to help you grow. By turning obstacles into opportunities, you'll build stronger problem-solving skills and develop confidence. Next time you face a challenge, don't stress; solve it like a boss!

PROBLEM-SOLVING WORKBOOK

Exercise 1: Problem Snapshot

Objective: Practice identifying and defining problems clearly.

1. Think of a recent personal challenge you faced.

Write the problem in one sentence.

_____
_____
_____

2. List three factors that contributed to this problem:

   a. _____

   b. _____

   c. _____

Reflection Questions

How did clearly defining the problem help you understand it better?

_____
_____
_____

What might you do differently next time when a problem arises?

_____
_____
_____

Exercise 2: Information Detective

Objective: Develop skills in gathering relevant information.

1. Choose a current challenge you're dealing with. Describe the challenge:

_____
_____
_____

2. List all the information you need to solve this problem.

_____
_____
_____

3. Identify where you can find this information (e.g., online, from friends, mentors):

_____
_____
_____

Practical Application

How will gathering this information help you better understand your challenge?

_____
_____
_____

Exercise 3: Brainstorm Bonanza

Objective: Enhance creative thinking by generating multiple solutions.

1. Take the problem you identified in Exercise 1. Describe it again in one sentence:

_____
_____

2. Set a timer for five minutes and brainstorm as many solutions as you can:

   a. _____

   b. _____

   c. _____

   d. _____

   e. _____

   f. _____

   g. _____

3. Review your list and highlight the three most promising ideas:

   a. _____

   b. _____

   c. _____

Reflection Questions

Which solutions surprised you the most?

_____
_____
_____

How does having multiple options make you feel about solving the problem?

_____
_____
_____

Exercise 4: Pros and Cons Chart

Objective: Learn to evaluate and compare different solutions.

1. From your top three solutions in Exercise 3, create a pros and cons list for each:

Solution 1:

Pros:
_____
_____
_____

Cons:
_____
_____
_____

Solution 2:

Pros:
_____
_____
_____

Cons:
_____
_____
_____

Solution 3:

Pros:
_____
_____
_____

Cons:
_____
_____
_____

2. After comparing, which solution seems best and why?

Exercise 5: Action and Reflection Journal

Objective: Foster continuous improvement through reflection.

1. Implement the solution you chose in Exercise 4. What solution did you choose?

Keep a journal for one week, noting your progress and any challenges. Write a daily summary of what happened:

Day1:

Day2:

Day3:

Day4:

Day 5:

_____
_____
_____

Day 6:

_____
_____
_____

Day 7:

_____
_____
_____

2. At the end of the week, summarize what worked, what didn't, and what you learned:
What worked?

_____
_____
_____

What didn't work?

_____
_____
_____

What did you learn?

_____
_____
_____

Reflection Questions

How did implementing your solution impact the problem?

_____
_____
_____

What would you do differently in the future based on your experience?

_____
_____
_____

This workbook is designed to guide you through the problem-solving process, helping you reflect on each step and build a toolkit of strategies you can use in real life.

Make Smart Choices Every Time
By Maurizia Mancini

Making decisions is about more than just listing pros and cons. It's about aligning your choices with your core values, trusting your intuition, and having faith in your ability to make the right call, even when it's hard. Smart decision-making requires self-awareness, confidence, and, sometimes, a leap of faith.

In this next section, we meet Jamie, who is faced with a difficult choice. She has an opportunity to take on a leadership role but is uncertain if she's up for the challenge. Will Jamie lean into self-trust and step forward? Let's see how she navigates her dilemma.

Jamie's Dilemma

Jamie sat on the edge of her bed, staring at the crumpled piece of paper in her hand. She had to make a decision, an important one. Her friend Sasha asked her to be the captain of their school's soccer team, but she wasn't sure if she was ready for the responsibility. She liked soccer and helping people, but being the captain seemed like a big deal—too big.

Her mom knocked on the door and peeked inside. "Everything okay, Jamie?"

Jamie sighed. "I don't know, Mom. I have to decide if I want to be the captain of the soccer team, but I just don't know what to do."

Her mom smiled and sat next to her. "You know, making decisions is a bit like being a detective. You have to gather clues, listen to different parts of yourself, and then figure out what feels right."

Jamie frowned. "Different parts of myself?"

"Yes," her mom continued. "Imagine your mind as having three parts. The first part is like the boss at the front desk—the conscious mind. This is the part of you that thinks, plans, and decides. It's where you make most of your everyday choices, like what to eat for breakfast or which socks to wear."

Jamie giggled. "So, the boss picked the rainbow socks today?"

"Exactly!" her mom chuckled. "Then, there's the subconscious mind. It's like a giant library that stores everything you have ever experienced: every sight, sound, smell, thought, and feeling. It's a bit like your personal detective's notebook. Even if you don't always remember these experiences, they still influence you."

Jamie thought for a moment. "So, like when I just know something but don't know why?"

"Yes! That's your subconscious at work. And finally, there's a third part called the super-conscious. Think of it as a wise owl sitting above everything, watching over both the boss and the library. The super-conscious always knows what's best for you. It's like an inner compass pointing toward what feels truly right."

Jamie nodded slowly. "But how do I know what the wise owl thinks?"

Her mom reached into her pocket and pulled out some blank pieces of paper. "Let's play a little game to find out."

The Decision Game

Jamie's mom handed her a pen and paper. "First, write your choices. You could write, 'Be the captain,' 'Don't be the captain,' and then one extra option with the word 'Other.' Fold them all up and mix them in a bowl."

Jamie did as her mom suggested, folding the papers tightly and dropping them into the bowl. "Okay, now what?"

"Close your eyes," her mom instructed, "and pick one paper. Don't open it. Just hold it in your hands."

Jamie picked one up and squeezed the paper gently in her palm.

"Now, without peeking, choose one and hold it in front of your heart. Keep your eyes closed and connect to it without reading it. How does it feel in your body? Is your stomach tight or relaxed? Are you smiling, or do you feel uncertain?"

Jamie closed her eyes tighter. She didn't know what was written on the piece of paper, but at first, she felt a little nervous, like when she stood in front of the class to give a presentation. Then, she felt a warm, exciting feeling in her chest, like when she saw her dog wagging its tail after school.

"I feel… good, I think," she said softly. "But I'm a bit scared, too."

"That's okay," her mom replied. "It's not just about finding a clear yes or no. It's about listening to your body and your feelings—your detective clues. That way, you're not just using your head but your whole self to decide."

"Now, pick one of the other pieces of paper."

Without reading it, Jamie picked a second one and closed her eyes. She didn't feel nervous this time but a little sad.

Jamie opened her eyes, left the folded piece of paper, and took the third, holding it in front of her heart without reading.

She felt nothing in particular.

"I think I'm done."

"Now, open your eyes and open the three pieces of paper. Look, the first was 'Be the captain.' Do you remember how you felt with it in your hands?"

"Yes! I was scared at first, but it was exciting! I liked that feeling!"

"What about the second?"

"It felt easier but also sad. I didn't feel that good."

"It sounds great, Jamie! You see, in this game, you are not looking for yes or no when blindly picking a piece of paper; you are looking for all the feelings and intuition. Then, you have more information and decide more easily!"

"I love it! I have a question, though. Why did we put the 'Other' paper among the options?"

Her mom smiled. "Sometimes, we think we only have two choices, but there might be options we haven't thought about yet. The 'Other' paper reminds us to stay open to new possibilities."

Jamie nodded, a little more confident now. "So, it's like checking with the boss, the library, and the wise owl before making a choice?"

"Exactly," her mom grinned. "Now, do you feel ready to make your decision?"

Jamie looked down at the folded papers and smiled. "I think I do."

In the end, Jamie discovered that making decisions isn't just about choosing an option, it's about connecting with how each choice feels and trusting her inner guidance. With her heart, mind, and intuition aligned, she realized that the answers she needed were already within her. Now, with confidence and clarity, she was ready to take the next step.

Learn from Mistakes Without the Pain
By Maurizia Mancini

Jamie was playing in her first soccer game as captain, and things were not going as planned. She made a few bad passes, and the team was losing by two goals. Her cheeks felt hot with embarrassment. She could hear some of the kids on the sidelines snickering.

After the game, Jamie felt like hiding. Then, she remembered something her coach once told her: "You can either say 'Oh, that's terrible!' or turn it into 'Let's make it bearable!'»

Jamie chuckled. *Okay, maybe that's not the exact saying, but close enough*, she thought.

She realized that everyone makes mistakes, even the most successful people. Jamie remembered how Thomas Edison, the inventor of the lightbulb, had tried thousands of times before he got it right. If he had given up after his first mistake, we might all be sitting in the dark right now.

The difference between a great leader and everyone else isn't that they never make mistakes. It's that they know how to use their mistakes to grow. Instead of being afraid of mistakes, great leaders see them as gifts—opportunities to learn something new.

Jamie sat down with her notebook and reflected on what happened in the game.

1. What went wrong? She wrote down everything that didn't go well. "I missed a pass," she scribbled, "because I wasn't looking."

2. Why did it happen? Then, she thought about why it happened. "I was nervous," she admitted. "I was too busy thinking about the crowd instead of the ball."

3. What did I need? Jamie noticed a need behind her mistake: "I needed to feel more confident."

4. What can I do next time? She decided to take a deep breath next time and focus on her teammates' movements instead of the crowd.

Jamie smiled. Mistakes weren't so scary when she broke them down like this. She remembered something her mom always said about forgiveness. In Italian, the word for forgiveness is "perdono," which means "per dono" or "as a gift." By forgiving herself, she gave herself a gift—a chance to learn and grow.

Exercise: Turn Your Mistakes into Gifts

1. Reflect on a mistake: Think of a mistake you made recently. Write what went wrong.

_____
_____
_____

2. Ask why: Why did it happen? Was there something you needed? Maybe you needed more information, more practice, or just a little more time.

_____
_____
_____

3. Give yourself a gift: Imagine forgiving yourself for the mistake. What can you learn from it? How can you grow from this experience?

_____
_____
_____

4. **Create a plan:** Decide one thing you will do differently next time. Forgiving yourself is a gift; it's like finding treasure in an unexpected place.

_____
_____
_____

Jamie knew that mistakes weren't failures but just steppingstones to becoming a better person and leader.

CHALLENGE WORKBOOK

Great leaders aren't just born; they grow and learn by facing challenges, making decisions, and reflecting on their mistakes. Here are some fun scenarios to help you practice turning mistakes into learning opportunities, making decisions, and becoming a confident leader!

Scenario 1: Finding Solutions to a Common School Problem

Challenge: Imagine there's a problem at your school. The lunch line is always too long, and some kids don't get enough time to eat. As a leader, how would you solve this problem? Lets explore:

1. **Identify the problem:** What exactly is happening? (Example: "Kids have to wait too long in line, and lunch breaks are too short.")

_____
_____
_____

2. **Brainstorm solutions:** Write at least three ideas that could help fix the problem. Don't worry if some ideas seem a bit silly; sometimes, the best solutions come from creative thinking.

- Solution 1:

   _____

- Solution 2:

   _____

- Solution 3:
  _____

3. **Choose the best solution:** Which idea do you think would work best? Why? Write your reasons. Remember to think like Jamie; consider how you feel about each option, like in the Decision Game.

   _____
   _____
   _____

4. **Plan your action:** How would you implement your solution? Who would you talk to, and what would you need to do? Write a step-by-step plan.

   _____
   _____
   _____

Scenario 2: Decision-Making Exercises Involving Real-Life Situations

Challenge: Imagine you're faced with a real-life decision. Read the scenario below and use the Decision Game method to figure out your best choice.

Situation: You have been invited to two different birthday parties on the same day. One party is for your best friend, and the other is for a new friend you really want to get to know better. You can't attend both.

1. **Your options are:**

   Option 1: Go to your best friend's party
   Option 2: Go to the new friend's party
   Option 3: Other (maybe you can think of a different idea)

2. **Feel it out:** Write in a piece paper each of the options above, fold the papers, and keep them in front of you. With your eyes closed, pick a piece of paper and hold it by your heart. If you don't have a paper with you, just close your eyes and imagine yourself being at each party or whatever you chose for option 3. How does your body feel? Are you excited, nervous, happy, or sad? Write what you notice for each option in each of these situations.

- Option 1 Feelings:
  _____

- Option 2 Feelings:
  _____

- Option 3 Feelings:
  _____

3. Decide: Based on how you felt, which option seems best for you? Why? Remember, it's okay to have mixed feelings—what's important is understanding them.

_____
_____
_____

Scenario 3: Reflections on Past Mistakes and Lessons Learned

Challenge: Think about a mistake you made in the past. Maybe you forgot to do your homework, or you accidentally hurt a friend's feelings. Use this exercise to reflect on what happened and learn from it.

1. Reflect on a mistake: Write a mistake you made recently. What happened? Describe the mistake.

_____
_____
_____

2. Ask why: Why did it happen? Was there something you needed at that moment (more time, better understanding, or a moment to breathe)? Write your thoughts.

_____
_____
_____

3. **Learn from it:** Imagine forgiving yourself for the mistake. Think about the Italian word "perdono" ("per dono"), which means "as a gift." What gift can you find in this mistake? What did it teach you? What did you learn?

_____
_____
_____

4. **Plan for next time**: Decide one thing you will do differently in the future. Write your plan and keep it somewhere you can see it often.

_____
_____
_____

By completing these scenarios, you'll be practicing real-life problem-solving, making better decisions, and learning how to grow from mistakes—just like the best leaders do. Remember, every challenge is a chance to learn and grow. Keep being curious, and never be afraid to try!

CHAPTER 5

TEAMWORK MAKES THE DREAM WORK

Why Working Together Is a Win-Win
By Susan Etter

Teamwork isn't just something parents, teachers, or coaches talk about; it's the key to achieving success in almost everything—whether you're managing a group project, solving tricky homework, or striving for a big win in sports. For teenagers stepping into leadership roles, understanding the power of teamwork can transform challenges into opportunities and create lasting connections with others. A win-win mindset is the key to unlock your leadership and fulfill your dreams and goals.

Think about a time when you were stuck on a homework problem. You tried everything, but it just wasn't clicking. Frustrated, you thought about giving up. Now, imagine you reach out to a friend or classmate for help. They explain it in a way that suddenly makes sense. Relief! You finish your work, and the stress is gone.

Here's the best part: both of you win. You got the support you requested, and the person helping you feels good for making a difference. This is the heart of teamwork—a win-win mindset that makes everything more effective and enjoyable.

Teamwork is powerful because it combines strengths. Maybe you're excellent at writing, while your friend is great at organizing. When you work together, the task becomes easier, often more creative, and resolved faster.

It also teaches you how to receive support. Asking for help isn't a sign of weakness; it's an opportunity to grow. Whether you're learning a new skill or tackling a big challenge, teamwork allows you to share the load and achieve better results. And let's face it—completing something as a team feels more rewarding than doing it alone.

One of the greatest gifts of teamwork is the connection it creates. When you combine each other's strengths and connect powerfully to each other, you develop trust and respect. You also learn faster, build new skills and the process becomes more enjoyable.

For example, working on a group project or playing on a sports team doesn't just accomplish the goal at hand. It also deepens friendships and builds bonds that can last for years. These connections become a support system for future challenges, making them easier to overcome.

Great leaders know that teamwork is essential. They bring people together, recognize individual strengths, and inspire collaboration. By creating a space where everyone can contribute, leaders ensure the entire team succeeds.

When you embrace teamwork, you're not just participating—you're learning the skills to become a leader yourself. Leadership isn't about doing everything alone; it's about empowering others to shine and working together toward a shared goal.

Teamwork isn't only about achieving goals—it's also about enjoying the process. Whether you're playing sports, solving homework problems, or finishing a project, working together makes the journey more fun and less stressful.

And when the work is done, there's more time to celebrate and enjoy the rewards with the people who supported you. Sharing wins and creating memories as a team makes success even sweeter.

The next time you encounter a challenge, remember: reaching out for support creates a win-win. By combining each other's strengths, you learn faster, build new skills, and deepen relationships. The process becomes more enjoyable, and the rewards feel greater when shared.

Teamwork makes the dream work, and the dream gets even better when everyone is winning.

Real Life Win-Win

To illustrate the power of teamwork and how it transforms challenges into victories I am going to share my daughter Emilie's story and my own experience. Let's learn some new ways of being and how teamwork in action made a difference for all by these stories.

When Emilie was in 8th grade, she played on her school's volleyball team. She loved the sport but struggled with one critical skill—getting her serves over the net. Instead of giving up or tackling the problem alone, Emilie built a small support team. She sought guidance from her coach and practiced daily with her best friend, Teresa, who encouraged her every step of the way.

Their teamwork paid off. Emilie's serves became consistent and reliable, boosting her confidence and helping her team score more points. By season's end, the entire team had grown stronger. Each member contributed something unique—skill, strategy, or support—and together, they achieved more success than they could have individually.

The Lesson

Emilie's story shows how teamwork turns challenges into collective victories. By seeking help and working together, she not only improved her confidence as a player but also built stronger relationships and a stronger team. Her experience is a reminder that no one has to face challenges alone. A team united in purpose and support is always stronger, proving that teamwork truly makes the dream work.

Like Emilie, I've faced challenges where teamwork made all the difference. My experiences with bullying—first as a teen and later as an adult—taught me the power of requesting support from others to overcome tough situations.

Bullied as a Teen

In 8th grade, I earned a spot on the cheerleading squad after an amazing tryout, landing a perfect front flip. But instead of celebrating, I was excluded by the other cheerleaders who were upset I had taken their friend's spot.

They gave me the wrong times for away games, told me to wear the wrong uniform, and made fun of me. I felt alone and hurt. Eventually, I left cheerleading behind and joined tennis and basketball teams, where I found acceptance, built lasting friendships, and experienced the power of supportive teammates.

Bullied as an Adult

Years later, at a class reunion, a classmate bullied me again, both verbally and physically. When I shared what happened, few classmates even a close friend didn't seem to care, and I felt abandoned and not supported. For the next reunion, fear almost stopped me from going. But this time, I reached out for support. Classmates listened, the committee assured me they would address the issue, and friends promised to stick by my side. Their support gave me the courage to attend, by being brave honest and in communication with others who could help me! The class reunion turned into a joyful night of connection and celebration. The win-win was: I was being powerful, and the classmates were enrolled, and we created a magical dreamy night together with memories for a lifetime.

The Lesson

From these experiences, I learned that teamwork transforms challenges into victories. As a teen, it helped me find my place. As an adult, it gave me the courage to face my fears.

When we work together, we create something stronger than any obstacle—a team that wins.

So, embrace the power of teamwork, and watch how it transforms your life.

WINNING TEAM WORKBOOK

This workbook is your step-by-step guide to building your dream team, achieving shared success, and deepening connections with others. Use the examples to inspire your answers and discover the power of teamwork in action.

Exercise 1: Pick Your Passion

Think of something you're passionate about—something you love and enjoy, like sports, theater, music, art, or dance.

My Example:

I love tennis.

Your Answer:

_____
_____
_____
_____

Exercise 2: Build Your Dream Team

Choose the people you want on your team. Write their names and explain why you picked them. What unique strengths or qualities do they bring?

My Example:

  I chose my grandchildren because they want to learn the game of tennis and how to play with others. They bring joy, excitement, and curiosity and inspire me to love the game of tennis more and more. They created a new connection for me. I was enjoying tennis again.

Your Answer:

1. _____
Why:

_____
_____
_____

2. _____
Why:
_____
_____
_____

3. _____
Why:
_____
_____
_____

4. _____
Why:
_____
_____
_____

5. _____
Why:
_____
_____
_____

Exercise 3: Create Greatness Together

Plan the specific actions your team will take to achieve your shared goal. Use your leadership and vision to organize the steps and create something meaningful.

My Example:

I chose tennis. My vision was to play the game with others instead of just watching matches on TV. I called my family members who love tennis and invited them to play with me at a local court. I set a date and time and brought extra rackets and tennis balls, and we made it happen. Game on!

Your Answer:
_____
_____
_____

Exercise 4: Ways of Being

Reflect on the qualities you embodied that helped you bring your team together. These are the ways of being that inspire success and connection. For instance, being bold, brave, adventurous, fun, playful, curious, loving and authentic.

My Example:

When I created a team for standing up to a bully, and also for attending my reunion being supported, I was being brave, courageous, vulnerable and intentional. This allowed me to face my fear which was keeping me a victim of someone else's bad behavior and nothing to do with who I am.

Your Answer:

1. _____
2. _____
3. _____

Exercise 5: Reflect on Results and Discoveries

Take a moment to reflect on the outcomes and lessons learned from your teamwork experience.

1. What results, connections, and relationships did you create through teamwork?

My Example:

I spent more time with people I love, created lasting memories of funny moments on the tennis court, and felt closer to my family.

Your Answer:
_____
_____
_____

2. What did you discover about yourself and others?

My Example:

I discovered how much I enjoy tennis and how teaching younger family members builds their confidence. I also realized that playing together as a team creates a sense of closeness, belonging, and joy.

Your Answer:
_____
_____
_____

3. What's next? What other teams or projects can you create as a leader?

Your Answer:
_____
_____
_____

Final Thoughts

Building a winning team is about bringing people together, recognizing each other's strengths, and having fun along the way. Teamwork creates opportunities to learn, grow, and build lasting relationships. Remember: when you work together, everyone wins!

How to Be the Best Team Player
By Julie Kaanapu

How to Be the MVP (Most Valuable Player) on Your Team

Do you know that one kid in your group project who did nothing? Yeah, we've all been there. The one who "forgets" to check the group chat or conveniently has the Wi-Fi break down the night before the project's due.

Spoiler: That's not the teammate you want to be.

Here's the thing about being on a team. Whether it's for a school project, sports, or organizing a pizza party (seriously, pizza parties need good teams), you get to be more than just "present." You get to *participate*. And being a great teammate isn't rocket science. In fact, it's kind of fun when you figure it out.

Let's Get Real: What Does a Great Teammate Actually Look Like?

A great teammate isn't just someone who checks the boxes and gets things done. They're the person who lifts everyone up and makes the whole team better.

Picture it like this: If your team were a pizza (yum, right?), a great teammate is the cheese that holds everything together. Sure, the pepperoni's flashy, and the crust is important. However, without that cheese, the whole thing would fall apart.

Now, think of the best teammate you've ever had. Someone who always seemed to make things work smoothly. Now, picture the *worst* teammate (ugh). What's the difference between them?

Seven Things Great Teammates Do, the Not-So-Great Ones Don't, and How You Can Become One

1. **They show up**: Not just physically but mentally. They're in it to win it.
2. **They communicate**: They don't let the group text die for three days straight.
3. **They do their part**: Whether designing a poster, making that tricky pass on the court, or bringing snacks, they deliver.
4. **They help others shine**: They pass the ball (literally and metaphorically). They support the team, not just themselves.
5. **They're adaptable**: Change always happens, and they don't let it freak them out or ruin their goals. They can shift quickly and see challenges as opportunities to keep the momentum going.
6. **They hold themselves accountable**: They take responsibility, don't place blame, and commit to improving things.
7. **They're fun to be around**: No one likes a complainer who brings the energy down, and everyone likes to be around someone who makes them feel good.

Let's break each of those down.

1. They show up—fully.

A great teammate isn't just physically present. They're mentally and emotionally engaged, too. Showing up means you're not sitting there daydreaming about what's for dinner while your group is trying to brainstorm ideas. It's about paying attention, participating, and being ready to contribute—whether at practice, in a group project, or during a meeting.

Example: Imagine you're at soccer practice. Everyone's running drills, but you notice one of your teammates seems tired and is falling behind. A great teammate would run alongside them, offer encouragement, or even suggest taking a water break. It's not about being the fastest runner; it's about being aware of your teammates' needs and stepping in to support them.

2. They communicate—a lot.

Have you ever been in a group where no one responds to messages, and you're left wondering if the project is still happening? That's a nightmare. Great teammates don't let communication fizzle out. They check in, send updates, and make sure everyone's on the same page.

Good communication doesn't just mean sending texts, either. It's about listening. A great teammate pays attention to what's *not* being said, too. Is someone holding back ideas? Are people stressed out? Asking questions and making sure everyone is heard is part of being a solid team player.

Pro Tip: Next time you're in a group setting, ask open-ended questions like, "What do you think?" or "What else could we try?" It encourages others to share their ideas, and you might uncover something brilliant.

3. They do more than their fair share.

Do you know what's better than doing your part? Going above and beyond. A great teammate doesn't stick to the bare minimum. They look for ways to help others and support the team. When you notice a teammate struggling with their role or behind on their part of the work, don't just shrug it off; step in and offer a hand.

Example: During a group science project, your part was to create the PowerPoint slides, but you noticed the research section was incomplete. Instead of ignoring it, you ask the person in charge if they need support and offer to help finish the research. That kind of effort makes people want to work with you again.

4. They encourage and uplift others.

Great teammates know that when the team does well, *everyone* shines. That means they don't hog the spotlight or get competitive in a negative way. Instead, they focus on uplifting others.

If someone's struggling, they offer support or give them credit when they do something awesome. Think of it like being a cheerleader for your team. It could be as simple as giving someone a high-five, complimenting their effort, or hyping them up before a big presentation or game.

Example: Jake is a basketball star who often hogs the ball. He was a star on his own, but the team got better when he started passing the ball and letting others take shots. He made sure others had their moments to shine, too. That's how you win—by making sure *everyone* has the chance to succeed.

5. They're adaptable.

No one likes the person who freaks out when plans change, or things don't go exactly right. A great teammate is adaptable and goes with the flow. Whether it's a last-minute project change, surprise challenge, or teammate dropping out, they stay calm and help find solutions instead of panicking.

Example: Imagine you're at a school fundraiser, and your original plan to bake and sell cookies gets shut down because someone forgot the ingredients (oops!). A great teammate doesn't sulk or blame others. Instead, they think on their feet. "Let's switch to selling raffle tickets or organize a quick game to keep things moving." They help the team pivot and keep going.

6. They hold themselves accountable.

A great teammate doesn't point fingers when things go wrong. Instead, they take responsibility for their actions, own up to mistakes, and work on fixing them. Accountability builds trust, and trust is the foundation of any successful team.

Example: If you missed a deadline or dropped the ball on a task, instead of making excuses, say, "Hey, that's on me. I'll work harder to make it right." This shows maturity, sets a good example for the rest of the team, and puts a play in action to rectify it.

7. They're fun to be around.

Finally, a great teammate brings good vibes. No one wants to be around someone who's always complaining or dragging the group down. Great teammates find ways to keep things light even when the pressure is on. Whether cracking a joke, keeping spirits high during a tough game, or playing music while you're working on a group project, a positive attitude is contagious.

Example: If your group project is dragging on and everyone's tired, instead of groaning, try cracking a joke, suggesting a quick break to recharge, or reminding the group of the hard work you've all put in and how far you've come. You can always find something positive and what's working well. Keeping the mood light makes it easier for everyone to keep going.

Real-Life Example: The Group Project (Dun, Dun, Dun)

Picture this: You're assigned to a group of four for your history class project. You have Sarah, who loves to overachieve (and let's face it, kind of takes over); Kyle, who vanishes after the first meeting; and Megan, who's constantly saying, "Whatever you guys want to do is fine with me." Then, there's you.

You have two choices.

Option A: You let Sarah take charge, complain about Kyle, and roll your eyes every time Megan shrugs.

Option B: You step up and make the team better. Maybe you take the lead on organizing tasks or encourage Megan to speak up because you know she's got great ideas (even if she's shy). And maybe, just maybe, you give Kyle a call to remind him he's still on planet Earth.

The project gets done in **Option A**, but it's a mess. Sarah's stressed out; Kyle is MIA (missing in action), and everyone's secretly mad at each other.

However, in **Option B**, you create a team that works together. Sarah doesn't feel like she has to do everything; Kyle is slightly less invisible, and Megan's ideas help elevate the project. You're not just coasting; you're *leading*.

BEST TEAM PLAYER WORKBOOK

Want to level up your team game? Here are some self-check questions:

1. Am I communicating enough? Did you ghost the group chat because your phone was on silent? Make sure you keep the team in the loop.

What can I do to become a better communicator?

_____
_____
_____

2. Am I doing my part? Have you done what you said you'd do? If not, why not? It's okay to ask for help, but don't leave your team hanging.

How can I ensure that what I say I'll do gets done?

_____
_____
_____

3. Am I supporting my teammates? Did you encourage someone else today? Sometimes, a simple "Great job!" or "Hey, can I help with that?" goes a long way.

What's something you can do daily to uplift someone else?

_____
_____
_____

Action Steps to Be an MVP Teammate

Here's how you can put it into action starting today.

1. **Show up with energy:** Next time you're in a group meeting or team huddle, be fully present. Don't sit in the back with your AirPods on. (We see you.)
2. **Ask questions:** A great teammate is curious. If you're confused or feel like something's off, ask questions. "Hey, how's everyone feeling about this?" is a great way to get the conversation going.
3. **Be responsible:** If something doesn't get done, own up to it. Don't point fingers (unless it's at yourself). Say, "That's on me; I'll fix it."
4. **Step up when it's hard:** If no one else is volunteering to take on that tricky task, be the one to do it. Trying counts for a lot, even if you're not an expert.
5. **Celebrate your team:** Don't walk away after a game or project. Say, "Good job, everyone!" Even if things didn't go perfectly, acknowledgment matters.

In a Nutshell

A great teammate is the glue that holds the team together. They show up ready to contribute, communicate openly, support others, and are responsible for their actions. They're adaptable, positive, and always looking for ways to lift the whole team up. If you want to be the kind of person people want on their team, practice these habits and watch your team transform into something unstoppable.

Keep the Peace: Solving Team Conflicts
By Mary Beth Lydon

Resolving conflicts peacefully and maintaining team spirit among friends, students, and teens can be challenging. This is because it takes students and teens who are committed, brave, and willing to step up and develop the leadership skills and strategies needed to resolve conflicts and maintain team spirit. Does the idea of becoming a leader light you up?

Leaders are special people who set themselves apart because they choose to do the right thing by helping others. Leaders do not judge others; rather, they view people, situations, and information through a lens of openness, curiosity, and neutrality. Being neutral means leaders do not attach a positive or negative meaning or emotion to a person, situation, or event. Leaders view others and situations without emotional attachment to a certain outcome or result.

Amazingly, leadership characteristics and behaviors can be developed by anyone, including you. This is exciting because it means you can become a leader with some practice. Leadership behaviors are typically modeled for students and teens by existing leaders in the community, like teachers and coaches, and their behaviors can be practiced and strengthened by students and teens throughout their lifetimes.

Student leaders are important in helping resolve conflicts that might arise anywhere in everyday life. Opportunities to resolve conflicts among students and teens can show up anywhere and everywhere—at home, school, school-sanctioned events, athletic events, and social and community activities and events.

Here are ten key strategies for teen leaders like you to practice to avoid and resolve conflicts successfully:

1. Encourage open communication.

- *Create a safe space:* Foster an environment where everyone feels comfortable expressing their thoughts and feelings without fear of judgment.

- *Use "I" statements*: Encourage everyone to share their feelings using "I" statements (e.g., "I feel upset when…"), which can help everyone involved express their feelings without placing blame.

2. Teach active listening.

- *Model listening skills:* Demonstrate how to listen actively by giving your full attention, nodding, and summarizing what the other person said.

- *Practice listening exercises:* Engage in activities or roleplaying exercises that focus on listening skills and empathy.

3. Set ground rules for discussions.

- *Respectful interaction:* Establish and reinforce rules for respectful behavior during discussions, such as not interrupting and avoiding name-calling.
- *Constructive criticism:* Encourage giving feedback positively and constructively, focusing on behavior rather than personal attributes.

4. Promote team-building activities.

- *Group projects:* Involve others in group projects or activities that require collaboration and problem-solving, which can strengthen your ability to work together.
- *Fun challenges:* Organize fun and engaging challenges that require teamwork and creativity, fostering a sense of camaraderie.

5. Encourage empathy.

- *Perspective-taking:* Use activities or discussions that help others understand different viewpoints and the impact of their actions.
- *Empathy exercises:* Share stories or scenarios and discuss how different people might feel in those situations.

6. Teach problem-solving skills.

- *Brainstorming solutions:* Guide others through brainstorming and evaluating different solutions to conflicts, emphasizing cooperation and compromise.
- *Decision-making practice:* Involve others in making decisions as a group, helping them learn how to negotiate and agree on solutions together.

7. Facilitate mediation and peer support.

- *Peer mediation:* Train interested students as peer mediators who can help their peers resolve conflicts in a neutral, non-judgmental, and supportive manner.
- *Mentorship:* Pair older students with younger ones for mentorship, allowing them to model positive conflict resolution behaviors.

8. Maintain a positive environment.

- *Celebrate achievements:* Recognize and celebrate individual and group accomplishments to build a positive and supportive atmosphere.
- *Encourage positivity:* Promote a culture of encouragement and kindness, reinforcing positive interactions and behaviors.

9. Provide guidance and support.

- *Adult supervision:* Ensure there are trusted adults, such as teachers, counselors, or parents, who can offer guidance and intervene when necessary.
- *Conflict resolution workshops:* Offer workshops or sessions on conflict resolution and emotional intelligence to build skills and understanding.

10. Model and reinforce positive behavior.

- *Lead by example:* Demonstrate respectful and empathetic behavior in your interactions with others.
- *Positive reinforcement:* Praise and reward positive conflict resolution efforts and teamwork to reinforce these behaviors.

The good news is that by practicing these ten strategies, you'll develop the leadership characteristics and skills needed to become a student leader, handle conflicts constructively, and maintain a positive and cooperative team environment at home, at school, and within your community.

Remember that effective teamwork starts with communication: listening to your teammates and speaking when necessary. Reliability is key; follow through on commitments and hold yourself accountable for your role. A positive attitude is essential, especially when things get difficult. Instead of pointing fingers, focus on solving problems together. Flexibility, being able to adapt to different personalities, and being willing to compromise for the team's good are also important. These are keys to keeping the peace and solving conflicts in a team. Don't forget to celebrate the team's successes, big or small, as this helps build trust and unity, and bringing solutions to a team in a peaceful way is a big win and a reason to celebrate.

Remember that a strong team needs everyone to show up and contribute. And you are a valuable member of any team you choose to be in. So play fair, peacefully, and full out. Your team is counting on you!

KEEP THE TEAM PEACE WORKBOOK

This workbook is designed to help teenagers understand and practice conflict resolution, empathy, and positive teamwork skills.

Exercise 1: Expressing Empathy Through a Short Play

Empathy is a key skill in resolving conflicts and strengthening relationships.

1. Write and perform a play: Work with a friend or on your own to create a short scene. Include two characters facing a disagreement or misunderstanding. One character should express empathy toward the other's feelings or perspectives during the conflict.

   _____
   _____
   _____

2. Reflect after performing: How did showing empathy impact the resolution of the conflict? How might expressing empathy help you in real-life situations?

   _____
   _____
   _____

Exercise 2: Understanding Team Dynamics and Your Role

Conflict often arises in groups due to misunderstandings or differing opinions. Reflecting on these moments helps develop stronger team connections.

1. Recall a recent group conflict: Write about a time when you experienced or witnessed a disagreement in a group setting (school project, sports team, friend group, etc.).

   _____
   _____
   _____

2. Analyze your role: How did you respond to the situation? What could you have done to mediate or support others if you stayed neutral?

   _____
   _____
   _____

3. Apply empathy: Imagine how you could have used empathy to ease the conflict. Write one or two sentences you could have said to show understanding of someone else's perspective.

_____
_____
_____

Exercise 3: Roleplaying Conflict Resolution

Conflict is a part of life, but how we handle it shapes our relationships and outcomes. Scenario Options (Choose One):

- Peer pressure to cheat on an exam.
- Disagreement over group responsibilities for a project.
- Argument with a friend over a rumor.

Steps:

1. Write or act out the conflict: Create a dialogue where the disagreement plays out. Show each character's perspective and feelings.

_____
_____
_____

2. Resolve the conflict: Use three strategies discussed in the chapter (e.g., active listening, expressing empathy, focusing on solutions). Demonstrate how the conflict can end positively, with all parties feeling understood.

_____
_____
_____

3. Reflect on responsibility: Answer these questions.

   What action helped resolve the conflict?

_____
_____
_____

How could you use similar strategies in your own life?

_____
_____
_____

What is your role as a team member in promoting peace and cooperation?

_____
_____
_____

Takeaway:

You can build stronger, more supportive relationships by practicing empathy and resolving conflicts effectively. These exercises help you develop leadership skills, enhance teamwork, and create a peaceful environment for everyone. Keep practicing, and you'll see how keeping the peace leads to better results for your team and yourself!

CHAPTER 6

TAKE CHARGE OF YOUR TIME

Master Time Like a Pro
By Winnie Napeñas

Have you ever felt like there aren't enough hours in the day to do everything you want? Maybe you have homework piling up, sports practice to get to, and friends who want to hang out, and you also want some time to just chill. It can feel overwhelming! However, here's a secret: The most successful people aren't just lucky; they're pros at managing their time. They know how to take charge of their day instead of letting the day take charge of them.

In this section, you will learn about mastering your time like a pro while making time for fun and play. By the end, you'll have the tools to take control of your schedule, prioritize what matters, and feel in charge of your day — all while keeping things fun and exciting. Are you ready? Let's dive in!

What Does It Mean to Take Charge of Your Time?

Taking charge of your time is all about being intentional with how you spend each minute of your day. Think of your time like a bank account. You only have so many minutes each day — 1,440 to be exact — and you can't get them back once you spend them. So, it's important to spend your time wisely.

When you master your time, you're not just doing more; you're doing the right things that make you happy, help you grow, and move you closer to your goals. Whether that's acing your next test, getting better at a sport, or having more time to relax, it all starts with how you use your time.

Why Time Management Matters

Good time management isn't just for grown-ups with jobs and long to-do lists. It's for everyone, especially you! When you learn to manage your time well, you:

1. **Feel more in control**: Instead of feeling like your schedule is running you, you'll start to feel like you're running your schedule.
2. **Reduce stress**: Knowing what to expect each day and having a plan helps you feel more relaxed and less overwhelmed.
3. **Make time for what matters**: You'll have more time for things you enjoy, like hanging out with friends, playing your favorite games, or practicing a hobby.
4. **Reach your goals faster**: Whether it's getting better grades, becoming a team captain, or saving for something special, good time management gets you there faster.

Time Management Tips: How to Be a Pro at Planning Your Day

So, how do you manage your time like a pro? Let's break it down into simple steps you can start using right away.

1. Prioritize like a pro.

Imagine you have a jar and need to fill it with big rocks, pebbles, and sand. If you start with the sand, there won't be room for the big rocks. However, if you put the big rocks in first, the pebbles and sand can fill the gaps. Think of your tasks like these rocks. The "big rocks" are the most important things you need to do, like studying for a test or finishing a project. The "pebbles" are less important tasks, like organizing your room. The "sand" is all the fun stuff, like playing video games or scrolling on your phone.

Pro Tip: Start your day with the "big rocks," the most important things. This way, even if you don't get to everything on your list, you'll have tackled the most crucial tasks.

2. Create a to-do list and use a planner.

Using a planner or an app can be a game-changer. Writing down what you must do daily helps you visualize your time and plan. Break down bigger tasks into smaller, manageable steps. Instead of writing "do science project," break it down into "research topic," "write outline," "create slides," etc.

Pro Tip: At the end of each day, spend five minutes writing a to-do list for tomorrow. This way, you wake up with a plan already in place.

3. Beat procrastination with the "Two-Minute Rule."

Ever find yourself putting off a small task that lingers in the back of your mind? The Two-Minute Rule, introduced by David Allen in his book Getting Things

Done, offers a simple solution: if a task takes two minutes or less to complete, do it immediately. Whether it's responding to an email, filing a paper, or putting away laundry, these quick wins create a sense of accomplishment and build momentum. By tackling the small things, you clear mental clutter and set yourself up for greater productivity.

Pro Tip: Break the bigger tasks into chunks and commit to working on them for just five minutes. Often, starting is the hardest part, and once you begin, it's easier to keep going.

4. Learn to say "No" without feeling guilty.

Your time is valuable, and you can't do everything. If a friend invites you out, but you have a big project due, saying no is okay. It doesn't mean you don't care; it means you're taking charge of your time.

Pro Tip: Practice saying, "I'd love to, but I have to focus on this right now. Can we hang out another time?" People will respect you for knowing your priorities.

5. Use breaks wisely: *The Pomodoro Technique* (Cirillo, 2006).

Have you ever tried studying for hours and felt like your brain was turning to mush? Developed by Francesco Cirillo, The Pomodoro Technique offers a practical way to maintain focus and prevent burnout. The method involves working for twenty-five minutes followed by a five-minute break. After completing four "Pomodoros," you take a longer break lasting fifteen to thirty minutes. This structured approach helps you stay sharp and allows your mind to recharge effectively.

Pro Tip: Use your five-minute breaks to stretch, grab a snack, or take a quick walk. Avoid screens during breaks to give your eyes and mind a rest.

6. Reflect and adjust.

At the end of each week, take a few minutes to reflect on how you spent your time. Did you meet your goals? Where did you waste time? What could you do better next week? This is how you keep improving and become a true time management pro.

Pro Tip: Celebrate your wins, no matter how small. Did you manage to finish all your homework on time? Awesome! Did you complete a project early? Great job! Recognizing your progress keeps you motivated.

Final Thoughts: You Have the Power to Take Charge

Mastering time management is like learning to ride a bike. At first, it might feel wobbly and awkward, but the more you practice, the easier it gets. Remember, it's not about being perfect. It's about making small changes that help you use your time better and feel more in control of your life.

By taking charge of your time, you're setting yourself up for success—not just in school but in everything you do. So, grab your planner, set those goals, and start managing your time like the leader you're destined to be!

Key Takeaways:

- **Prioritize** tasks by focusing on the most important ones first (the "big rocks").
- **Plan your day** with a to-do list or planner.
- **Avoid procrastination** by using the "Two-Minute Rule."
- **Learn to say "no"** to protect your time.
- **Use the Pomodoro Technique** to balance work and rest.
- **Reflect and adjust** your approach weekly for continuous improvement.

You've got this. Now, go out there and make the most of your time!

TIME MANAGEMENT WORKBOOK

Exercise 1: Create a weekly schedule.

Take a blank sheet of paper or use the templates below to create a schedule for the week. Block out time for school, homework, and sports, and don't forget to include downtime. This will help you see where your time is going and make adjustments.

Step 1: List your priorities (big rocks).

Before filling in your schedule, list the most important things you need to do this week.

- **Priority 1 (Big Rock):**

_____

- **Priority 2 (Big Rock):**

_____

- **Priority 3 (Big Rock):**

_____

Step 2: Fill out your weekly overview.

Fill in the table below with your daily activities, including school, homework, sports, and other commitments. Don't forget to include time for yourself; fun and relaxation are important, too.

Time	Monday	Tuesday	Wednesday	Thursday	Friday	Saturday	Sunday
6:00 AM							
7:00 AM							
8:00 AM							
9:00 AM							
10:00 AM							
11:00 AM							
12:00 PM							
1:00 PM							
2:00 PM							
3:00 PM							
4:00 PM							
5:00 PM							
6:00 PM							
7:00 PM							
8:00 PM							
9:00 PM							

Exercise 2: Set and track your short-term and long-term goals.

Write one short-term goal (something you want to achieve this week) and one long-term goal (something bigger, like making a team or saving for a new gadget). Break these goals into small, manageable steps, and track your daily progress.

Short-Term Goal:
_____
_____

Long-Term Goal:
_____
_____

Exercise 3: Reflect on time-management habits and areas for improvement.

At the end of the week, look back. Write your answers to the questions below and adjust for next week:

What went well with your time management? (Did you balance work, school, and fun well?)
_____
_____
_____

What areas could you improve?
_____
_____
_____

What distractions kept you from reaching your goals?
_____
_____
_____

This reflection will help you improve week after week. Keep practicing and learning; soon enough, you'll have more time for what matters most to you!

Take Charge of Your Time and Own It
By Emily Villagomez

Time management might sound like a boring lecture from a teacher, but it's a superpower that can set you apart as a leader. Whether it's balancing school, sports, or social life, taking charge of your time means taking charge of your life. Let's dive into a story that shows how owning your choices and learning from them can turn things around when it feels like everything is slipping through the cracks.

The Story of Sam and the Missed Assignment

Sam was a high school junior who was juggling school, work, sports, and hanging out with friends. Like many teens, he felt like there weren't enough hours in the day to get everything done. He loved playing basketball with his team, and weekends were all about hanging out with his friends and playing video games. However, things started to pile up.

One Monday afternoon, after a long practice, Sam got a notification on his phone: "English Essay Due Tomorrow." Sam's heart sank. He had completely forgotten about the essay. He'd spent the weekend at a skateboarding competition and hadn't thought once about schoolwork. The essay was a major grade, and he hadn't even started.

Sam could already imagine his teacher's disappointment, and the thought of failing the assignment made him anxious. Still, instead of getting to work right away, he spent an hour scrolling through YouTube shorts, telling himself he'd start after dinner.

When dinner came and went, Sam finally sat down with his laptop. He stared at the blank page but was so tired from practice that he couldn't focus. The deadline was creeping closer. Sam started thinking of excuses he could give his teacher, or maybe he could skip school tomorrow to avoid facing it. However, deep down, he knew the only way to fix this was to take responsibility for his choices.

Sam took a deep breath, put his phone in another room, and told himself, "No more distractions." He powered through the essay, making the best of the time he had left. It wasn't perfect, but he got it done.

The next morning, Sam handed in his essay with relief but knew he needed a better strategy to manage his time. He promised himself that next time, he'd plan ahead. After all, he didn't want to be in this stressful situation again.

Learning from the Moment: Owning Up and Moving Forward

When Sam got his essay back, the grade was okay—not great—but he realized something more important. His teacher said, "I can tell you rushed through this, Sam. I know you're capable of something better." Instead of getting defensive, Sam nodded. He knew she was right. He stayed after class to talk to her and asked for advice on balancing his workload.

His teacher gave him tips on managing time better, like breaking big projects into smaller tasks and using a planner to stay on top of things. Sam also admitted that he had procrastinated. It wasn't easy to own up to it, but his teacher appreciated his honesty and willingness to learn.

From that point on, Sam committed to prioritize his work. He started using a planner, setting reminders, and planning ahead. He even told his basketball coach that he needed to spend some extra time after school to catch up on assignments. It wasn't easy, but taking responsibility for his choices made Sam feel more in control.

Final Thoughts: Responsibility is Power

Sam's story is a reminder that leadership isn't just about leading others; sometimes, it's about leading yourself. Taking ownership of your actions, whether it's schoolwork, sports, or friendships, builds trust and confidence. When you're responsible for your time and choices, you become more reliable to others and yourself.

Being a leader means stepping up, even when it's hard, and learning from mistakes. Like Sam, you don't have to be perfect, but you do need to take responsibility for your actions. The more you own it, the better you'll get at managing your time and rocking everything you set out to do.

So, whether it's an essay, a project, or something else, remember that the best leaders are the ones who can admit when they've slipped up and take steps to improve. You've got this. Now, go out there and take charge!

RESPONSIBILITY WORKBOOK

Exercise 1: Take a moment to reflect and think about a time when you had a responsibility and did not manage your time well. What were the consequences of your time management? Were there times that you avoided or put off the responsibility? How did you feel about the outcome? What lesson did you learn after the experience?

_____
_____
_____

Exercise 2: Your Responsibility Planner

Now it's your turn to create your own responsibility plan! This will help you identify what area you can take responsibility, set a clear goal, and outline a step-by-step plan to achieve it. You've got this!

Step 1: Break it Down

List a responsible goal you get to complete (e.g., a project, homework, athletic goal etc.).

Break it into smaller steps.

Task	Step 1	Step 2	Step 3	Step 4	Deadline
Example: Write Essay	Research Topic	Write Draft	Edit Essay	Submit	Jan 15th 2024

Step 2: Eliminate Distractions

Distractions are inevitable when you're working toward a goal. The key is learning to overcome them and stay focused on what truly matters.

Write down two distractions you might face and how you will avoid them.

- Distraction 1: _____ → How to Avoid: _____
- Distraction 2: _____ → How to Avoid: _____
- Distraction 3: _____ → How to Avoid: _____

Step 3: What Daily Habits Can You Adopt to Meet This Goal Responsibly?

Think about simple actions you can take each day to stay on track.
Examples: setting reminders, scheduling time to focus on homework.

Habit 1: _____
Habit 2: _____
Habit 3: _____

Step 4: Accountability Buddy

When working toward a goal, having someone who supports you and holds you accountable can make a big difference in staying on track and achieving success. Who can you share your plan with to keep you accountable?

Write the name here: _____

Make sure to check in with your buddy regularly so you can complete your goal in a timely fashion and celebrate.

Step 5: Celebrate

It is time to celebrate! After each goal is completed, take a moment to acknowledge your victory. Celebrating your accomplishments, no matter how small, boosts your motivation and reinforces positive habits you have built up.

What are you going to do to celebrate the completion of your goal?

_____
_____

Step 6: Review

After the celebration. You get to go back and see what worked in your leadership and what didn't so you can double down on the actions and habits that worked and shift from those habits and actions that did not.

What worked in your completion of this goal? Were you effective with your time? Did you keep yourself connected with your buddy and accountable to your goal?

_____
_____
_____

What didn't work in your completion of this goal? Did you fall back on a step? Did you get distracted? How can you take action so next time you have a goal you are responsible for your time and your choices?

_____
_____
_____

Final thoughts

Remember we all make mistakes. The important thing is to learn from them and grow. By reflecting on your experiences, you can become an effective leader taking ownership of your actions and build trust in yourself. You've got this!

Setting Your Sights on Success
By Diocelina Love

As a young leader, you're ready to make a difference, but have you ever set a goal only to feel overwhelmed or unsure where to start? You are full of potential, energy, and ideas, yet none of that gets you far without a clear vision. Remember how, earlier in this book, you read about the power of vision? Your vision is like the north star; it keeps you on track when distractions or challenges come your way. Goals are the steps that guide you toward that vision. Just like a GPS recalculating when you make a wrong turn, setting goals keeps you moving forward even when life throws unexpected detours, and that is how you set your sights on success.

Leaders don't just talk about what they want; they create a plan and go after it. However, setting goals isn't just about writing down some things you want to do. It's about being intentional, focused, and accountable. Whether you want to ace your next test, make the varsity team, or save money for something big, the goals you set today build the foundation for your future success.

Let's look at why setting goals is essential for you right now. First, goals give you direction. They help you break your big vision into smaller, manageable steps. Second, goals motivate you. When you see progress, it inspires you to keep going. And third, goals build confidence. When you accomplish something, no matter how small, you prove to yourself you can do it. That's what being a leader is all about—taking charge of your life, one goal at a time.

For teens, setting goals can mean things like improving your grades, stepping up your game in sports, developing new skills, or even building better relationships with friends and family.

Whatever your goals are, it's important to make them SMART!

SMART is an acronym that stands for Specific, Measurable, Achievable, Relevant, and Time-bound; by Doran, G.T. (1981). By setting SMART goals, you'll create a clear roadmap to achieve your dreams. Imagine having a step-by-step plan to succeed in school, sports, or your favorite extracurricular activity. SMART goals help you stay focused, motivated, and confident.

What Are SMART Goals

SMART goals are designed to provide clarity, focus, and motivation. Each letter in SMART represents a criterion for effective goal setting

- Specific: Define your goal as clearly as possible. Instead of saying, "I want to be successful," say, "I want to increase my study time to 2 hours a day for the next 2 weeks."

- Measurable: Quantify your goal. If the progress can't be tracked, it's hard to know if you're on the right path. For example, "I want to complete five school projects each month."

- Achievable: Make sure your goal is realistic and attainable. Challenge yourself, but don't set yourself up for failure. For instance, "I want to learn a new language in two months" might not be achievable, but learning a new language in six months could be.

- Relevant: Ensure the goal is aligned with your vision and values. Ask yourself, "Why is this goal important to me?" It may not be worth pursuing if it's not tied to a bigger purpose. For instance, challenging yourself to learn a new language in six months that is tied to the vision of traveling to another country to communicate with family members you have never met is an important goal rather than just learning another language. You get to use your infinite imagination to create your vision and goals.

- Time-bound: Set a deadline. Deadlines create urgency and help you stay focused. For example, "I want to raise my math grade from a C to an A by studying an extra hour every day for the next six months.

As a young leader, you're ready to shine! The path to leadership starts with setting your vision and backing it up with clear, powerful goals. SMART goals help you create a clear plan to achieve success. So, take a moment to think about what you want to achieve. Write your goals, map out a plan, and get ready to crush them. Every step you take brings you closer to becoming the leader you're meant to be.

SMART GOALS WORKBOOK

Use this workbook to guide you step-by-step through the goal-setting process and to develop the discipline and vision to reach your targets.

Your Personal Goal Setting

Use the following space to identify a goal you want to work on and craft it using the SMART framework. You can set multiple goals—one at a time—or use this process for different areas of your life, like school, sports, or hobbies.

Goal Example

Goal: "Improve my math grade from a C to a B+ by the end of the semester."

Specific: I want to increase my math grade by studying thirty minutes a day.

Measurable: I will track my progress through test scores and homework grades.

Achievable: I will ask my teacher for additional resources and seek tutoring when needed.

Relevant: This goal will help me build a stronger foundation for future classes.

Time-bound: I aim to achieve this goal by the end of the semester (specific date).

Now, it's your turn.

Your Short-Term Goal

Goal:

Specific:

Measurable:

Achievable:

Relevant:

Time-bound:

Tracking Your Progress

Now that you've set a SMART goal, let's create a plan for tracking your progress. Regular check-ins will keep you focused and help you adjust your plan as needed.

Weekly Check-In

What did I accomplish this week toward my goal?
___
___
___

What challenges did I face, and how did I overcome them?
___
___
___

What's one thing I can improve next week?
___
___
___

Am I still on track to reach my goal by the deadline? If not, what adjustments do I need to make?
___
___
___

Reflect and Revise

Reflection is key to growth. Sometimes, you'll meet your goal, and sometimes, you'll learn from the process. It's an opportunity to see what worked and what didn't work and create something new and shift. Either way, reflecting on the journey and celebrating your effort is important.

End-of-Goal Reflection Questions

Did I reach my goal? Why or why not?
___
___
___

What worked well for me?
___
___
___

What did I learn about myself in the process?

_____
_____
_____

If I didn't achieve my goal, how can I adjust and try again?

_____
_____
_____

Celebrating Success

Write one way you'll celebrate your success when you reach your goal. It could be as simple as treating yourself to something you enjoy or taking time to reflect on your growth.

_____
_____

Long-Term Goal Setting

Your SMART goals can be steppingstones to something bigger. Now that you've learned how to set and achieve short-term goals, let's discuss long-term ones.

Long-Term Goal Example

Goal: "Graduate high school with honors."

Specific: I will maintain a 3.5 GPA or higher.

Measurable: I will track my grades each semester and aim for a balance between academics and extracurriculars.

Achievable: I will dedicate time each day for homework, set priorities, and seek help when needed.

Relevant: Graduating with honors will help me gain scholarships and get into the college of my choice.

Time-bound: I will achieve this by the time I graduate high school.

Your Long-Term Goal

Goal:

Specific:

Measurable:

Achievable:

Relevant:

Time-bound:

Staying Motivated

Getting off track is easy when working toward a goal, but staying motivated is key to success.

Here are some tips to help you stay focused:

- **Visualize your success.** Imagine how great it will feel to achieve your goal.
- **Break it down.** Big goals can feel overwhelming, so break them into smaller, manageable steps.

- **Find an accountability partner.** Having someone check in with you can keep you on track.
- **Celebrate progress.** Every small win is a step closer to the finish line.

Final Thoughts

Remember that your goals are like the GPS that helps you navigate the road ahead. Every goal you set and step you take brings you closer to the leader you are becoming.

You have the power to shape your future by setting goals and working steadily toward them.

Remember, it's not just about reaching the finish line, it's about the growth you experience in the journey. The progress is in the process. As you grow, you get to stand firm and uphold your values to ensure a future that is bright and filled with opportunities. Now, go out there and start achieving your goals, lead with purpose, and be all that God created you to be!

CHAPTER 7

GO WITH THE FLOW

Stay Cool: The Power of Adaptability
By Mary Beth Lydon

Growing up is fun, but let's face it, it can be hard sometimes. We all face challenges that threaten to take our focus away from what's important in our lives if we are not adaptable. These challenges might even cause us to stop all forward growth and momentum in our lives. This might look like not preparing for high school or college entrance exams, not adequately studying for final exams, or not showing up and being true to our word when we said we would do something for someone else.

Embracing adaptability is essential for everyone, especially for students and teens facing the ups and downs of growing up. Here are ten key ways to cultivate adaptability and stay cool whenever challenges arise in your life:

1. **Encourage a positive attitude about change.**

   - *Frame change as an opportunity:* Shift your thinking and view changes and challenges as opportunities for growth rather than threats. Share examples where change led to positive outcomes.

   - *Reinforce flexibility:* Recognize that flexibility is a valuable skill that can lead to new experiences and possibilities.

2. **Teach problem-solving skills.**

   - *Break down challenges:* Practice breaking down problems into smaller, manageable steps, which makes adapting possible solutions easier.

   - *Explore multiple solutions:* Brainstorm various solutions to a problem and weigh the pros and cons to find the best approach.

3. Promote self-awareness and reflection.

- *Encourage journaling:* Keep a journal to reflect on your experiences, thoughts, and feelings; this will help you understand your responses to change.
- *Discuss lessons learned:* After encountering a challenge, discuss what was learned from the experience and how you can apply those lessons in the future.

4. Foster resilience and persistence.

- *Celebrate effort:* Recognize and praise your efforts and perseverance, not just successes. This reinforces the value of persistence.
- *Share stories of resilience:* Share stories of individuals who have overcome adversity, highlighting their adaptability and perseverance.

5. Develop emotional regulation skills.

- *Practice coping strategies:* Teach and practice coping strategies, such as deep breathing, mindfulness, or positive self-talk, to manage stress and emotions.
- *Encourage emotional expression:* Create a safe space for you to express your feelings and discuss how to cope with difficult emotions.

6. Encourage healthy routines and self-care.

- *Balanced lifestyle:* Practice a balanced lifestyle that includes regular exercise, healthy eating, and adequate sleep, which support overall well-being and adaptability.
- *Routine and flexibility:* Establish routines, but also emphasize the importance of being flexible with these routines as needed.

7. Promote curiosity and open-mindedness.

- *Explore new interests:* Explore new hobbies and interests, which helps you become more open to new experiences and change.
- *Respect diverse opinions:* Foster an environment where you learn to respect and consider different viewpoints and ideas.

8. Model adaptability.

- *Lead by example:* Demonstrate how you handle change and unexpected situations in your life. Show how to adapt positively and solve problems effectively.

- *Share personal experiences:* Talk about times when you had to adapt and how you managed the situation, including both successes and challenges.

9. Encourage seeking support.

- *Ask for help:* Normalize seeking help from friends, family, or mentors when facing difficulties. Ask for support and resources.
- *Utilize resources:* Encourage yourself to take advantage of available resources, such as school counselors or online tools, for guidance and support.

10. Facilitate growth opportunities.

- *Challenge yourself:* Seek opportunities to step out of your comfort zone, such as taking on new responsibilities or participating in unfamiliar activities.
- *Reflect on growth:* Reflect on your growth and achievements from these challenges to reinforce your adaptability and confidence.

By fostering these habits, you can develop a strong sense of adaptability that will help you stay cool as you navigate the challenges and changes in life and remember to celebrate your growth and successes as you become adaptable to change.

Bounce Back Stronger: Building Resilience
By Sue B Johnson

Life as a teenager is filled with challenges, changes, and unexpected moments. Whether it's dealing with school pressure, navigating friendships, or working through personal struggles, you're constantly being tested. But here's the thing: It's not about avoiding challenges but learning how to face them head-on and grow through the experience. That's where resilience comes in; it's your inner strength, your ability to keep going even when life doesn't go as planned.

Resilience is a key trait for any leader. It helps you stay grounded and focused even when things get tough. As a young leader discovering the potential inside of you, building resilience will allow you to face setbacks with confidence and keep pushing toward your goals. Resilience isn't just about staying strong; it's about bouncing back stronger, learning from what went wrong, and becoming more adaptable in the process.

Resilience is like a muscle: The more you use it, the stronger it gets. When we build resilience, we learn how to overcome obstacles, manage stress, and keep going even when things get tough.

John's Story: A Lesson in Resilience

John had always loved the idea of acting. So, when auditions for the school play were announced, he signed up immediately. John spent hours practicing lines and imagining himself on stage under the bright lights. He felt ready—until the day of the audition.

John stepped onto the stage, heart pounding, but suddenly forgot his lines. His mind went blank, and he could feel the eyes of the teachers and other students on him. John stumbled through the rest of the audition, barely making it to the end. When he walked off the stage, John felt embarrassed and defeated.

John thought to himself, *I completely messed up. Maybe I'm not meant for this. I should just quit.*

For days after the audition, John avoided talking about it. He started to believe he wasn't good enough for the part—or any part, for that matter. However, deep down, John knew he didn't want to give up.

The Turning Point: A Teacher's Advice

One afternoon, John's theater teacher, Mr. Parker, noticed his change in behavior. He pulled John aside for a chat.

Mr. Parker said, "John, I could see you were disappointed after the audition, but you know what? Setbacks like these don't mean it's over. They're just part of the journey. Everyone stumbles at some point. It's how you bounce back that matters."

John responded, "But I forgot all my lines. I don't think I'll ever be good enough for this."

Mr. Parker exclaimed, "You will be if you keep trying. Resilience isn't about getting it perfect every time; it's about picking yourself up, learning from what went wrong, and coming back stronger."

This conversation changed the way John thought about the audition. Instead of seeing it as a failure, John began to view it as a learning experience. He realized that resilience wasn't about never facing challenges but about how he responded to them.

Determined to improve, John decided to give it another shot. Even though he felt nervous about the audition results, he knew he could still grow as an actor. John asked Mr. Parker for advice on how to stay calm during auditions. Mr. Parker gave John some breathing exercises to practice before stepping on stage and encouraged him to focus on enjoying the process, not just the result.

With renewed focus, John practiced, memorized his lines, and learned to manage his nerves. He worked hard to improve his acting skills and stayed after school to rehearse. John felt a little more confident every day, knowing he was building resilience step by step.

A few weeks later, John heard about auditions for another play. This time, John felt a mix of excitement and nerves but reminded himself of the lessons he had learned. Resilience taught John that he didn't need to be perfect; he just needed to give his best and not let setbacks define him.

When it was John's turn to audition, he felt the familiar nerves creeping in. However, this time, he took a deep breath, just like Mr. Parker had taught him, and focused on enjoying the moment.

John delivered his lines with confidence, and even though he made a small mistake, he didn't panic. Instead, John kept going just like he'd practiced. After the audition, he felt proud, not because everything went perfectly but because he didn't let fear hold him back.

John didn't get the lead role, but he was cast in a supporting part—a part he never would have gotten if he'd quit after the first audition. More importantly, John learned that resilience is about persistence. Every challenge, every stumble, is a chance to grow stronger.

John thought *I didn't get the lead, but I'm proud of myself. I faced my fears and bounced back. Next time, I'll do even better.*

John realized that he could apply resilience to any area of life, not just acting. Whether in school, friendships, or future challenges, John knew he had the strength to keep going no matter what.

Resilience Matters for Leadership

Leadership isn't just about leading others; it's also about leading yourself. The best leaders are those who can stay calm under pressure, make decisions when things are tough, and bounce back when they face setbacks. Resilience is what allows leaders to keep pushing forward even when the path is uncertain.

As you grow, you'll face many situations where resilience will be key. Whether it's managing a group project at school, dealing with a personal challenge, or working toward a big goal, resilience will help you succeed. Just like John learned on stage, resilience gives you the strength to keep going, no matter what.

The Power of a Growth Mindset

One of the most important lessons John learned was the value of a growth mindset—the belief that abilities can be developed through effort and learning. Instead of thinking he wasn't good at acting, John learned to think he could get better if he kept trying. This shift in perspective is crucial for resilience.

A growth mindset helps you see failure not as the end but as part of the journey. When you view challenges this way, you're more likely to keep pushing forward even when things are difficult. Every time you bounce back from a challenge, you're building resilience and preparing yourself to take on even bigger challenges in the future.

Conclusion: Bouncing Back Stronger

Resilience doesn't mean never facing difficulties. It means having the courage to face those difficulties and the strength to come back even stronger. Like John, you have the power to build resilience and bounce back from any challenge life throws your way. Each setback is a chance to grow, and you become a little stronger every time you rise.

The next time you face a tough situation, remember: You can bounce back. You can grow stronger. Resilience is within you, waiting to be developed. Keep going and growing with the flow. You've got this!

RESILIENCE WORKBOOK

Flexibility and Resilience Challenges

Exercise 1: Reflect on a time you adapted to a new situation.

Journal exercise: Take five minutes to write about a situation that required you to unexpectedly change your expectations or change what you were doing or going to do in favor of doing something else. Reflect on how the unexpected change made you feel. Reflect on the results of the change. Reflect on the lessons learned. Identify one to three positive outcomes from this unexpected change.

_____

_____

_____

Exercise 2: Create a resilience-building action plan.

1. **Self-awareness and emotional intelligence activity**: Keep a daily mood journal, noting events that triggered strong emotions and how you responded. How did these emotions impact your decisions?

Reflection: What emotions did you feel today? How did those emotions influence your actions?

_____

_____

_____

2. **Developing positive thinking activity**: Understand positive affirmations by writing down three things you like about yourself or three strengths you have.

   Reflection: How does focusing on your strengths make you feel?

   _____
   _____
   _____

3. **Problem-solving and critical thinking activity**: Think about real-life scenarios (e.g., peer pressure, balancing school and personal life) and develop a list of possible solutions.

   Reflection: What problems have you recently solved? How did you come up with your solution?

   _____
   _____
   _____

4. **Building confidence through challenges activity**: Set up a "Challenge of the Week" where you push your comfort zone (e.g., presenting in class or trying a new hobby). Debrief after each challenge to discuss how it felt.

   Reflection: What challenge did you face this week? How did you overcome it, and how did you feel afterward?

   _____
   _____
   _____

5. **Developing a growth mindset activity**: Learn the differences between fixed and growth mindsets. Reframe a recent negative experience with a growth mindset perspective.

   Reflection: How can you see a challenge as an opportunity to grow rather than something negative?

   _____
   _____
   _____

6. **Cultivating gratitude activity**: Start a gratitude journal where you write three things you're thankful for every day.

   Reflection: How does writing what you're grateful for change your mood?

   _____
   _____
   _____

7. **Encouraging self-compassion activity**: Write a letter to yourself as if you were your best friend, offering encouragement after a challenge.

   Reflection: How can being kind to yourself help when things are hard?

   _____
   _____
   _____

Turn Tough Times into Triumphs
By Carmen Orellana

Life isn't always smooth sailing; sometimes, it can feel like you're stuck in a storm. However, even when things are tough, turning those challenges into amazing achievements is possible. Let's dive into three inspiring stories of people who faced difficulties head-on and came out stronger than ever.

Story 1: Maya's Mountain Climb

Maya loved climbing trees in her backyard but dreamed of climbing the biggest mountain she could find. Maya was excited and nervous when her family planned a trip to climb a real mountain. The mountain was steep and challenging, and Maya found herself struggling. At one point, she wanted to give up because it was just too hard.

However, Maya remembered her dad's advice: "Every big challenge starts with a small step." She decided to take it one step at a time. Slowly but surely, she climbed higher and higher. When she finally reached the top, she was exhausted but overjoyed. Maya learned that perseverance and patience could help her achieve her dreams, no matter how tough the journey seemed.

Story 2: Liam's Art Show

Liam loved drawing and painting. He worked hard to prepare for his school's annual art show. He spent weeks perfecting his painting, but something went wrong when the big day came. A few days before the show, his painting accidentally got juice spilled on it. Liam was devastated. His painting was ruined, and he felt like giving up on the art show.

However, Liam's art teacher encouraged him to try again. Liam took a deep breath and started a new painting. He used the experience as a chance to be creative and explore new techniques. On the day of the art show, his new painting was a hit. People admired his creativity and resilience. Liam realized that even when things go wrong, he could find a way to make them right and grow from the experience.

Story 3: Emma's Soccer Game

Emma was excited about her first big soccer game. She practiced a lot but missed a crucial goal during the game and felt like she let her team down. Emma was upset and worried that she wasn't good enough.

After the game, Emma's coach talked to her about what happened. He reminded her that making mistakes was part of learning and improving. Emma decided to keep practicing and focus on her skills. Over time, she got better and became a key player on her team. Emma learned that failure is just a steppingstone to success, and with hard work and a positive attitude, she could turn her setbacks into victories.

In conclusion, Maya, Liam, and Emma faced challenges but didn't let those tough times stop them. Instead, they turned their difficulties into opportunities for achievement and triumph. Remember, whenever you're facing something tough, you have the power to overcome it and come out even stronger. Just like Maya, Liam, and Emma, you can turn tough times into triumphs with a little perseverance and a lot of heart.

CHAPTER 8

LEAD BY EXAMPLE

Actions Speak Louder than words: Be, Do, Have
By Keia Eden Lavine, HHP.

As a teenager, it may often feel like adults are constantly telling you what to do. Teachers, parents, coaches, and other authority figures seem to have endless advice about how to behave, what choices to make, and which path to follow. Let's be real; it can be frustrating, especially when their actions don't align with their words.

I vividly remember a moment from my teenage years that drove this lesson home. My dad was giving me one of those lectures about how I should act. He meant well, but it was hard for me to take him seriously. My dad often struggled with his temper and sometimes drank publicly. As a frustrated teenager, I pointed out the inconsistency between his words and actions. His response? "Do as I say, not as I do."

Those words made me so angry. They've stayed with me ever since, not as wisdom but as a reminder of how much actions matter. That moment taught me an important lesson: *Trust is built through actions, not words.* Even though my dad meant well with his advice, his inability to lead by example made it impossible for me to fully respect or emulate him. I didn't just want to hear what to do; I needed to see it.

I knew then that actions speak louder than words—and that is what I strive to emulate now every day: to let my actions speak for themselves.

This isn't unique to my experience. For many people, trust is earned through what someone does, not what they say. It's why we value integrity in leaders and role models. It's also why systems like the judicial process are built on evidence and actions, not accusations or empty promises. Watching adults whose actions didn't align with their advice taught me to question their trustworthiness. And without trust, how could I respect or follow their guidance?

Does this story sound familiar? Maybe there's someone in your life who says one thing but lives another. It's frustrating, isn't it? That's because, deep down, we know that true leadership isn't about what someone says; it's about what they do. Real leaders inspire others through their actions, not just their words.

As Benjamin Franklin wisely said, "Well done is better than well said." Leadership is not about commanding change but about demonstrating the values, actions, and character you hope to inspire in others. Let these words really sink in: *What you do has a far greater impact than what you say.*

Steven Covey, renowned *author of 7 Habits of Highly Effective People*, beautifully captures this idea, reminding you that every action you take matters; it impacts the lives of those around you. True leadership is rooted in integral action.

Think about someone in your life who has earned your trust through their actions. What did they do to make you believe in them? How did their actions inspire you to follow their lead? Leadership is built on these moments when people demonstrate their values in real and tangible ways.

When you lead by example, you inspire others to follow, not because they have to but because they want to. It's your daily choices and behaviors that earn their trust and respect.

Your choices and behavior become your character, and true leadership happens when your character is tested, allowing your actions to speak leadership.

When I was younger, a test of my character happened when I was tempted to steal some money from a wallet I found. My mom helped me through this dilemma by sharing a quote by C.S. Lewis: "Integrity is doing the right thing, even when no one is watching." It took me a while to understand what she meant, but those words stayed with me. I ultimately chose to turn the wallet in. True character isn't about what you say or how you present yourself to others. It's about who you are when no one is watching.

Your actions reflect the person you choose to be in the world, no matter the circumstances. Integrity means living in alignment with your values, even when no one is around to hold you accountable. It's about ensuring your actions validate your words.

Imagine finding a wallet full of money on the ground. What would you do? Would you turn it in if no one was around? Would your choice change if your friends or an adult were watching? What would you do if a friend asked you to lie for them? What if you saw a classmate cheating on a test? Would your response be different if no one was watching? How do your choices reflect your values when there's no one there to applaud or criticize you?

These moments of decision reveal our true character. John Wooden, one of the greatest basketball coaches in history, echoes the same sentiment: "The true test of a man's character is what he does when no one is watching." As a leader, your actions, both public and private, define you. They set the standard for how others see you and, more importantly, how you see yourself. The courage to do the right thing all the time is *leadership*.

Living by your values is easy when everything is going smoothly. But what happens when life gets tough? The true test of leadership comes during moments of adversity when your actions are the clearest reflection of who you are.

Think about it: When challenges arise, it can be tempting to let frustration, disappointment, or exhaustion take control. Maybe a friend ignores your text, and it stings. Or you have a rough day at school and feel completely unmotivated. Perhaps someone wrongfully accuses you of something, leaving you feeling misunderstood and defensive. In moments like these, it's easy to act out of emotion rather than principle.

But here's the truth: Every great leader faces challenges. The difference lies in how they respond.

Nelson Mandela once said, "I never lose. I either win or learn." This perspective reminds us that challenges are not just obstacles to overcome; they are opportunities to grow, demonstrate resilience, and lead with integrity. Your response during difficult times speaks volumes about your character and values. What you do matters far more than what you say you believe.

When life feels overwhelming, your actions can become powerful statements of who you are. Consider these moments as opportunities to lead by example, even if it feels small:

- **When you're tired, show up anyway.** Your decision to follow through, even when you're drained, tells others that commitment matters to you.

- **When someone upsets you, choose patience and kindness.** Responding with grace shows that you prioritize relationships over pride or anger.

- **When everything feels overwhelming, take one small step forward.** Small actions, even in chaos, demonstrate courage and perseverance.

These choices may seem insignificant at the moment, but they build a reputation of reliability, integrity, and strength over time. People notice when you keep showing up, even when it's hard. They see your consistency, and that builds trust.

The Principle of "BE, DO, HAVE:"

Leadership is built on a simple but powerful principle: "Be, do, have." This concept, popularized by Stephen R. Covey and rooted in ancient wisdom, teaches us that who we are shapes what we do, and what we do creates what we ultimately have.

1. **BE**: Your character, values, and mindset form the foundation of everything. It's about showing up as someone who is trustworthy, kind, courageous, and authentic, even when no one is watching.

2. **DO**: Your actions get to align with your character. What you do reflects who you are. Consistency between your values and your behavior is what builds trust and respect.

3. **HAVE**: The results, success, relationships, and influence are the natural rewards of living in alignment with your values and actions.

Many people think, *Once I have the resources or opportunities, I'll be able to do the right things and become the person I want to be.* However, "Be, do, have" flips that mindset. Start by being the person you aspire to be, and the rest will follow.

Daily Practice

Leadership isn't a one-time achievement; it's a daily commitment to align your actions with your values. Your actions are your most powerful tool for inspiring others and creating change.

As you go about your day, ask yourself:

- How can I lead by example today?
- What values do I want my actions to reflect?
- Who can I inspire simply by showing up and being my best self?

Remember, people may forget what you say, but they'll never forget what you do. Leadership starts with you. It's not about waiting for others to change; it's about becoming the example that inspires others to follow.

INSPIRATION WORKBOOK

Inspired to Inspire

1. Can you think of a time when you saw someone set a great example through their actions? What did they do, and how did it inspire you to try it yourself?

_____
_____
_____

2. Have you ever noticed someone copying something you said or did? How did it make you feel to realize your actions influenced them?

_____
_____
_____

3. What is one skill or talent you're proud of that you enjoy teaching or sharing with others? Why do you think it's important to pass it on?

_____
_____
_____

4. Think about your daily habits and personality. What are three traits or qualities you consistently show that you hope others—like siblings, friends, or classmates—will admire and adopt?

_____
_____
_____

Now, go and live your leadership through your actions and inspire others to do the same!

Be the Change: Setting a Great Example
By Erin Atwood

Imagine being the leader who inspires others to be their best selves. That sounds awesome, right? But what does it take to be that kind of leader? To create real change, you must lead by example. Living with integrity, kindness, reliability, and resilience lays the foundation for others to trust and respect you. Every choice you make sets a powerful example, creating a ripple effect that can impact your immediate circle and potentially many more.

Great leaders show others what to do by living the values they want others to follow. It's about setting the tone through your actions, whether being honest, kind, or dependable. When you lead by example, you inspire those around you to follow your lead and become better versions of themselves.

"Be the change you wish to see in the world" isn't just a saying; it's a powerful truth. Leadership starts with you, and when you embody the values you want others to follow, you become a living example of the change you're striving to create. You don't have to wait for the right moment or for others to act first. Being the change means stepping up, showing up, and influencing others through your consistent actions.

What Does It Mean to Be the Change?

Being the change means embodying the qualities you want to see in the world, like kindness, honesty, or courage. It's not about grand gestures but about showing up as your best self in everyday moments. Leadership isn't something you turn on only when it's convenient; it's how you live daily. Every decision you make, word you speak, and action you take can model the behavior you hope to inspire in others.

For example, if you value honesty, be honest in all your interactions. If you want to see more kindness, lead with compassion in everything you do. Change begins within, and the more you live out your values, the more you'll inspire others to follow.

Integrity: The Core of Being the Change

Being the change starts with integrity. Integrity means doing what's right even when no one is watching. It's about staying true to your values and being consistent in your actions. According to a study by the Josephson Institute, 93 percent of teens believe honesty is essential for leaders. This statistic highlights how crucial integrity is in leadership. Whether it's admitting when you're wrong or following through on a promise, integrity is the foundation of authentic leadership.

When you act with integrity, people trust you. Trust is crucial because leadership relies on it. Without trust, no one will follow your lead. By showing that your actions match your words, you build credibility and inspire others to be accountable in their lives.

How to Be the Change with Integrity

- **Be honest:** Speak the truth even when it's difficult. Being transparent builds trust and sets a high standard for others.

- **Own your mistakes:** Everyone makes mistakes. What sets leaders apart is their willingness to take responsibility and learn from them.

- **Stay consistent:** Be the same person in private as in public. Consistency in your actions shows people that you're reliable and trustworthy.

Kindness: A Powerful Way to Be the Change

Kindness is often underestimated as a leadership trait, but it has the power to transform environments and relationships. When you treat others with respect and compassion, you create a ripple effect. Your acts of kindness, whether big or small, can inspire others to do the same. This is how change spreads—one kind gesture at a time. Research by the Random Acts of Kindness Foundation shows that kindness can significantly increase happiness and well-being—not just for the receiver but also for the giver. Creating a culture of kindness fosters an environment where everyone feels appreciated, leading to stronger relationships and a more cohesive team.

When you're the change through kindness, you show that leadership isn't about being tough or controlling. It's about creating a space where people feel valued and appreciated. Kindness fosters connection and encourages others to follow your example.

How to Be the Change with Kindness

1. **Be kind to yourself:** Kindness isn't just about how you treat others; it's also about how you treat yourself. Being kind to yourself means a few things:

    - Seeing your worth
    - Being patient with your mistakes
    - Taking care of your physical and mental health
    - Forgiving yourself when you make mistakes

2. **Practice active listening:** Show you care by really hearing what others have to say. Listening builds trust and understanding.

3. **Offer help:** Don't wait for someone to ask; if you see a need, step up and help. Small acts of service show you're paying attention and willing to support others.

4. **Encourage others:** A few positive words can make a big difference. Genuine compliments or encouragement can lift someone's spirits and motivate them to do better.

Reliability: The Backbone of Being the Change

Being reliable means people can count on you. When you're the change, you don't just talk about it; you consistently show up and follow through. People trust dependable leaders who keep their promises and contribute their best in every situation. Your reliability sets a standard that others want to meet. According to a study by the Pew Research Center, 75 percent of teens value reliability in leaders. This indicates that when you demonstrate reliability, you build a foundation of trust and respect that encourages collaboration and teamwork. Your commitment to being dependable sets a powerful example for those around you.

Being reliable isn't about perfection; it's about consistency. You become someone others look to when things get tough because they know you won't let them down. This level of trust is built over time, and it strengthens your ability to influence and inspire.

How to Be the Change with Reliability

- **Follow through:** If you commit to something, do it. Whether it's big or small, following through shows that you take your commitments seriously.
- **Be consistent:** Show up in the same way day after day. Consistency builds reliability, and reliability builds trust.
- **Take responsibility:** When things don't go as planned, own it. Taking responsibility for outcomes, good or bad, shows maturity and leadership.

Staying True to Your Values

Leadership isn't always easy. There will be times when you face peer pressure and fear of judgment or criticism. However, being a leader means staying true to your values even when it's difficult. There will be moments when doing the right thing makes you stand out, but that's where courage comes in. Staying firm in your beliefs, even in the face of challenges, is what sets true leaders apart.

You may face situations where peer pressure makes it tempting to go along with the crowd. In those moments, remember that real leadership is about doing what's right even when it's not popular. It takes courage to stand up for your values, but that's what defines great leadership.

The Ripple Effect: Your Change Inspires Others

When you live the values you believe in, you create a ripple effect. The way you show up, embodying integrity, kindness, and reliability, can influence others in ways you might not even see. Your consistent actions set off a chain reaction, encouraging others to act in the same way. Being the change means recognizing that your influence extends far beyond yourself.

Your actions today can inspire someone tomorrow. The change you start within yourself doesn't just stop with you; it spreads. By being the change, you create a legacy of leadership that impacts everyone around you.

Remember, leadership begins with you. When you *be the change*, you show others what's possible. You're setting the standard for others whenever you act with integrity, show kindness, or are reliable. Change doesn't happen overnight, but through consistent actions, you have the power to transform your world. Be the change and watch how your leadership sparks change in others.

BE THE CHANGE WORKBOOK

Exercise 1: Leadership Values

List three values you believe make a good leader (e.g., honesty, kindness, reliability).

_____
_____
_____

Write one way you can show each of these values this week.

_____
_____
_____

Exercise 2: Integrity in Your Life

Think of a time when you acted with integrity. How did it make you feel?

_____
_____
_____

Write one way you can practice integrity today.

_____
_____
_____

Exercise 3: Kindness Challenge

List two small acts of kindness you want to create.

_____
_____
_____

Write one kind thing you can do for yourself.

_____
_____
_____

Exercise 4: Reliability Check

Write about a time you followed through on a promise. How did others respond?

_____
_____
_____

Choose one commitment this week and make sure to follow through.

_____
_____
_____

Exercise 5: Positive Impact

Write about one positive action you've taken recently. How did it affect others?

_____
_____
_____

What kind of leader do you want to be? Write your answer below.

_____
_____
_____

Spread the Vibes: Inspiring Friends and Peers
By Fabiola Baylon

Did you know true leaders aren't just about giving orders or taking control? Real leadership is about having a vision that lights people up and inspires them to want to be a part of it. It's not about doing everything yourself; it's about bringing others along on the journey, showing them the possibilities, and giving them the tools to help make it happen. Think of it like this: Your vision is a spark, and your leadership is what fans that spark into a flame by enrolling others in your passion.

When we look at some of the biggest accomplishments in history, none of them happened because of just one person. It always took a team working together toward a shared vision to turn dreams into reality. Leaders understand this. They know that to create something great, everyone needs a role. It's about building a future where people feel like their contribution matters and where they are empowered and inspired to make things happen alongside you.

What's amazing is that you can be that kind of leader, too. It's not about being the oldest, smartest, or most experienced. It's about knowing what you stand for, sharing that vision in a way that excites people, and inspiring others to believe in it with you. When you empower others by enrolling them in your vision, suddenly, you're not just one person; you're part of a movement that can accomplish big things.

The Power of Vision in Everyday Leadership

As a young leader, you have a unique opportunity to create change right where you are, whether in middle school or high school. You get to have a powerful vision, stay committed to it, and make decisions that align with it. What's exciting is that this isn't just something "older" leaders do. You can be an inspiration to your friends and peers right now.

Let's imagine you're in middle school, and you're chosen as the commissioner of a club, whether it's a school spirit club, a cultural group, or even a book club. This is your chance to bring a fresh vision to the table. Maybe your vision is to make your school's spirit day more inclusive or to create a club where students from different backgrounds can share their traditions and stories. The key here is that you get to be creative. You can show up with ideas that reflect who you are and what you believe in, and you can encourage others to carry them out with integrity.

Let's say you're leading a Cultural Appreciation Club. Your vision might be to create an environment where students from different cultures feel seen and heard. As a leader, you organize events like cultural food days, performances, or even a culture fair where students showcase their heritage. Your role isn't just about planning these activities; it's about getting your peers excited to participate, sharing their experiences, and helping others feel like a part of something bigger. You show up, align your actions with your vision, and invite others to join you.

As a leader, it's also important to give people a voice. Leaders aren't about dictating but listening and incorporating everyone's ideas. When your club members feel heard, they'll be more motivated to act, whether it's through voting on new ideas, helping you make decisions, or coming up with creative ways to engage more students. Suddenly, your club isn't just something you run; it becomes a team effort, and that's where the magic happens.

From Club Representative to School President

Let's take it one step further. What if your success in the club inspires you to run for student body president? You've already led your club, shown you can bring people together, and created real change. Now, you're ready to step up and represent all the school's clubs. As president, you continue to spread your vision of unity, inclusion, and connection. You inspire students to get involved by voting for initiatives, running for office, or participating in events that reflect the school's goals. The cool part is you're not only leading, but you're also creating an environment where everyone feels empowered to take part.

And your leadership doesn't have to stop at school. Imagine growing your impact beyond the campus—maybe getting involved in community projects, helping plan city events, or even leading youth initiatives at a state level. Your vision can expand as big as you want it to as long as you stay committed, keep inspiring others, and lead with integrity.

Your Leadership Journey Starts Now

Remember, leadership is about who you are and how you show up for others. It's about inspiring people to see the possibilities and empowering them to join you in making them real. Whether you're leading a club, running for student government, or helping organize an event, your vision and actions have the power to spread beyond the school walls, impacting your community and beyond.

Your journey as a leader starts with spreading the vibes and inspiring friends and peers to take action and work together, showing them they can be a part of something bigger. You don't have to wait to lead. It's about being present, having the courage to stand up for what you believe in, and inspiring others to come along for the ride. Are you ready to spread the vibes? Let's go!

SPREADING LEADERSHIP WORKBOOK

This workbook is designed to help you reflect on your leadership style, discover how you can set a positive example, and spread the vibes by encouraging your peers.

Exercise 1: Reflect on a time you led by example.

Think back to a moment when you stepped up and led by example. Maybe it was in a club at school, during a group project, or even within your group of friends. Leading by example means you show others what it looks like to act with integrity, passion, or responsibility.

Instructions:

Write about a time you led by example. What was the situation, and how did your actions influence others?

_____
_____
_____

How did it feel to be a leader at that moment? What did you learn from the experience?

_____
_____
_____

Reflection Questions

What specific actions did you take that set an example for others?

_____
_____
_____

How did those around you respond to your leadership?

_____
_____
_____

What would you do differently if you were in a similar situation again?

_____
_____
_____

Exercise 2: Commit to three actions that set a positive example.

Now that you've reflected on your past leadership, it's time to think about how you can continue to lead by example. Leadership doesn't always mean big actions; it can be found in everyday decisions. Whether it's staying true to your word, showing kindness, or stepping up when others hesitate, these small actions make a big difference.

Instructions:

List three actions you can commit to in the next month that will set a positive example for others. These get to be specific, actionable steps that you can take regularly.

_____
_____
_____

Why did you choose these actions, and how do you think they will impact those around you?

_____
_____
_____

Example Commitments:

1. I will help others feel included by inviting new people into my group activities.
2. I will speak up when I see someone being treated unfairly.
3. I will stay focused during group projects and encourage others to do the same.

Exercise 3: Write a letter of encouragement to a peer.

Part of spreading the vibes as a leader is supporting and uplifting those around you. When you encourage others, you create a positive and motivating environment where everyone can succeed. Think of a peer who could use some encouragement, whether they're facing a challenge, working on a project, or simply needing a reminder they're doing great.

Instructions:

Write a letter of encouragement to a peer. Be specific about what you admire about them and how you believe in their potential. Focus on how they've shown leadership qualities or how they can continue to grow into their strengths.

Letter Structure

- Start with a warm greeting and acknowledge something positive you've noticed about them.
- Share your encouragement, offering support for their current efforts or challenges.
- End with a motivating statement, reminding them they have the power to achieve their goals.

Reflection: How Will You Lead Going Forward?

Now that you've reflected on past leadership moments, made a commitment to set a positive example, and encouraged a peer, take a moment to think about how you'll continue to lead going forward.

Reflection Questions

What does leadership mean to you after completing these exercises?

_____
_____
_____

How can you continue spreading the vibes of leadership in your school, community, or personal life?

_____
_____
_____

What will you do differently to inspire others and make an even greater impact?

_____
_____
_____

Leadership is about action and inspiration. Whether through small acts of kindness or larger commitments, you have the power to lead by example and spread the vibes to those around you. Keep reflecting, keep growing, and continue to be the kind of leader who inspires others to follow their paths with confidence and courage.

CHAPTER 9

MAKE A DIFFERENCE IN YOUR COMMUNITY

Why Helping Others Feels Awesome
By Winnie Napeñas

Imagine you're walking through your neighborhood and notice a group of kids struggling to carry heavy boxes for a charity event. Without hesitation, you rush over to help them. As you lift the boxes, you notice the smiles of relief on their faces, and suddenly, you feel a warm glow inside. That feeling is the joy of making a difference.

Feel Good by Helping: The Helper's High

Helping others is one of the most powerful things you can do to make a difference. It doesn't just change the lives of those you help; it changes your life, too. This section is about understanding why helping others feels so good and how you can start positively impacting your community today.

Did you know that helping others can actually make you happier? Researchers have found that acts of kindness trigger the release of endorphins, the brain's "feel-good" chemicals. These are the same chemicals released during exercise, giving you a natural boost of energy and happiness. This phenomenon, often referred to as the "helper's high," was first introduced by Allan Luks in his book The Health and Spiritual Benefits of Helping Others, and further explored by Peggy Payne in her work on the positive effects of helping others. It's a scientifically backed reason why acts of kindness leave us feeling so amazing—and why lending a hand can benefit both the giver and the receiver.

However, it's not just about feeling good at the moment. Helping others can also boost your self-esteem, make you feel more connected to your community, and even reduce stress. It's like a superpower you didn't know you had.

When you help someone, you create a ripple effect, no matter how big or small the act. That one act of kindness can inspire others to do the same, creating a chain reaction of positive change. For example, let's say you volunteer to help clean up a local park. Your actions might inspire your friends to join you, and together, you make the park a better place for everyone to enjoy. Plus, seeing the results of your hard work—like a litter-free park—can make you feel proud and accomplished.

Every great movement in history started with just a few people who decided to make a difference. When you help others, you're contributing to something bigger than yourself. You're making your community a better place, one small act at a time.

Your community is like a big puzzle, and every person is a piece of that puzzle. When you step up to help, you're filling in a piece that might have been missing. Maybe a neighbor needs help with their groceries, or a local animal shelter could use an extra hand. Whatever it is, your efforts matter.

Helping others isn't just about solving problems; it's also about building connections. When you help someone, you show them that they're not alone and they matter. This creates a sense of belonging and strengthens the bonds in your community.

Ways to Make a Difference

You don't need to be a superhero to make a difference. There are plenty of simple ways you can help right in your community. Here are a few ideas to get you started:

- **Volunteer your time:** Whether it's helping at a local food bank, tutoring younger students, or cleaning up a public space, volunteering is a great way to give back.
- **Start a fundraiser:** If there's a cause you're passionate about, like animal welfare or helping the homeless, consider organizing a fundraiser. You could sell homemade crafts, hold a bake sale, or even set up a donation drive.
- **Be a friend:** Sometimes, the best way to help is just to be there for someone who needs it. Whether it's listening to a friend who's going through a tough time or helping a classmate with their homework, small acts of kindness can have a big impact.
- **Organize a community event:** Get your friends together and plan a fun event, like a neighborhood cleanup day or a charity car wash. You'll not only be helping but also have a blast doing it.

How to Start Today

Starting today is easier than you think! Here's how you can take action right now:

1. **Look around you:** Start by noticing what's happening in your immediate surroundings. Is there someone who could use a helping hand? Maybe a friend needs some encouragement, or a neighbor needs help with their garden. Start with something small that you can do today.

2. **Ask, "How can I help?"** Sometimes, the best way to know how to help is simply to ask. Talk to people in your community—your family, friends, teachers, or local organizations—and ask if they need anything or how you can get involved.

3. **Use your talents:** Everyone has something special to offer. Think about what you're good at, whether it's art, sports, writing, or organizing events, and find a way to use that talent to help others. For example, create uplifting posters for a local event if you're great at drawing. If you're good at math, consider tutoring a younger student.

4. **Make it a habit:** Helping doesn't have to be a one-time thing. Decide to do one kind act every day, no matter how small. It could be as simple as holding the door for someone, complimenting a classmate, or picking up litter you see on the street. The more you practice kindness, the more it becomes a natural part of who you are.

5. **Spread the word:** Encourage your friends and family to join you in your efforts. Share your experiences with them and invite them to volunteer with you. When more people get involved, the impact becomes even greater.

Making a difference in your community isn't just about helping others; it's about becoming the best version of yourself. When you take action to improve the lives of those around you, you're also growing as a person. You're learning the importance of empathy, responsibility, and leadership.

Remember, every act of kindness adds up—no matter how small. So, what are you waiting for? Start today. Look around, ask how you can help, use your talents, and make it a habit. The world needs more people like you!

Lead Cool Community Projects and Leave a Positive Mark in the World.
By Keia Eden Lavine, HHP.

As a teenager, I often felt powerless, overwhelmed by the demands of life: school, chores, maintaining friendships, and avoiding the drama in classroom cliques. On top of that, I was keenly aware of the world's big issues—racism, war, poverty, and famine. I'd find myself wondering, *How could I ever make a difference?* I felt small, as if my voice didn't matter. My friends and I joked that there wouldn't be a world left by graduation, but deep down, we feared it might be true.

Then, I met a mentor who changed everything for me. She wasn't famous. She wasn't a world leader or a social media influencer. She was just an ordinary person, but she showed me that small actions could create big waves of positive change. Her mentorship wasn't flashy; it was just a few hours spent with me here and there, but her impact taught me so much. She showed me how actions matter and how anyone can make a difference.

Inspired by her example, I decided to act. I started small, organizing a weekly community event where I read to kids at Starbucks. It was fun, and it gave me confidence. Over time, I realized that even small efforts could have a powerful impact.

From there, I kept hosting car washes, organizing painting groups, planning open mic nights, and eventually creating women's circles that met each month for empowerment. Each event brought people together, fostering connection and joy in a world that often feels divided. It was leadership, and it inspired others to join my cause and support the continuation of these things. I got to be a part of something greater than myself as women came from all over to participate and thank me for creating the space. And more importantly, it was fun!

If you've ever had an idea for something fun, like a day at the park, or noticed a need in your community, such as homelessness, or wanted to help a stray dog, now is your chance to step up and be the leader you are meant to be. Maybe there's something that bothers you, like graffiti or litter in your neighborhood. This is your invitation to do something about it.

Leaders don't wait to be told what to do. They see a need, set an intention, and take action.

By starting a community project, you can make a difference while developing your leadership skills. All it takes is choosing to get started. Imagine being the person who organizes a local park cleanup, starts a charity drive, or creates a neighborhood garden. This is about learning how to take an idea and turn it into a reality that benefits your community.

If you've ever struggled with doubt, remember that everyone is capable of great things. The key is taking action and being the change. Perhaps you might think making a difference is something only adults do, but teens around the world are proving otherwise.

Take Ravi Vora, a thirteen-year-old from Illinois. He founded the Hunger Halt initiative to combat food insecurity in his community. By organizing food drives and working with local food banks, Ravi has helped provide food to families in need.

Or consider Kailey Kornhauser, a fourteen-year-old from Oregon. Passionate about protecting the environment, Kailey started the Save Our Forests campaign. She organizes tree-planting events and community cleanups to raise awareness about deforestation and biodiversity.

These teens started with small ideas and big hearts, showing that age doesn't limit your ability to lead change. Take a moment to think about what matters most to you. Is it the environment, social justice, animal welfare, or something else? Why does this matter to you? Do you think about it often? Do you wish there was something you could do? If there was something you could do, what would it be? If you could cause change in this area, what would that mean to you? How would this change impact your community, school, or neighborhood?

Every great leader starts somewhere, and your journey begins here. This is your invitation to step into leadership. Like my mentor used to say, it only takes one to start a movement. So, I invite you to take this opportunity to start now. *Take action and be the leader you are meant to be.*

Through these seven steps, you can develop your own community project, create impact, and inspire others to join you in a passion-driven community impact project that matters to you and will make a difference.

1. **Live from your passion:** Passion is the spark that ignites meaningful change. What are you deeply passionate about? Maybe it's protecting the environment, helping people in need, or advocating for animal rights. Passion fuels your energy and commitment, making the work feel exciting rather than overwhelming. When you work from your passion, others can see your enthusiasm and are more likely to join and support your cause.

    Ask yourself: What excites you? What do you think about often? What would you dedicate your time to even if it wasn't required?

2. **Find the gap:** Look around your community, school, or neighborhood. Where do you see a need? What issues or challenges align with your passion? Finding the gap is about identifying opportunities where your efforts could fill a void or solve a problem. It could be something big, like addressing homelessness, or something smaller but impactful, like organizing a recycling program at school.

    Examples:

    - Is there litter in local parks?
    - Are there students in your school who feel isolated or left out?
    - Are local families struggling to access resources?

3. **Set goals:** Once you've identified a need, it's time to set clear goals for what you want to achieve. Goals give your project direction and help you measure progress. They can be as ambitious or modest as you like—what matters is taking steps toward a meaningful impact.

Tips for goal setting:

- Use the SMART method—Specific, Measurable, Achievable, Relevant, Time-bound (as mentioned on page 76)
- Break big goals into smaller, actionable steps
- Celebrate milestones along the way

4. **Create a plan:** Every successful project begins with a well-thought-out plan. Think about the steps you need to take to achieve your goals. Consider what resources, tools, or people you'll need. Will you need to contact someone for permission or support? A clear plan will help you stay organized and confident.

    Key elements of your plan:

    - **Tasks:** What needs to be done, step by step?
    - **Timeline:** When will you complete each step?
    - **Team:** Who can help you, and what roles will they play?
    - **Resources:** What supplies, tools, or spaces do you need?

5. **Take action:** This is where your leadership truly shines. Once your plan is ready, start taking the steps to bring it to life. Remember that leadership is about doing—not just talking about ideas. Your actions will inspire others and create tangible change.

    Tips for taking action:

    - Start small if necessary. Momentum builds over time.
    - Stay flexible. Problems might arise, but you can adapt.
    - Keep your focus on the impact you want to create.

6. **Inspire others:** Leadership isn't just about your actions; it's about bringing others along on the journey. Share your vision and explain why your project matters. When others see your passion and commitment, they're more likely to get involved and support your cause.

    Ways to inspire others:

    - Use social media to spread the word.
    - Talk to friends, classmates, or family members about your project.

- Create a sense of excitement and purpose by showing how their involvement can make a difference.

7. **Leave a legacy:** True leadership creates lasting change. Think about how your project can continue to have an impact even after it's finished. Can someone else take it over? Will it inspire others to start similar initiatives? A legacy doesn't have to be massive; it just needs to leave the world a little better than you found it.

   Reflect on your legacy:

   - How will your project improve your community in the long term?
   - Who else can you inspire to carry on the work?
   - What lessons did you learn that you can share with others?

Remember: *The power of one person is unstoppable when fueled by passion and action.* You have what it takes to make a difference.

Now, it's your turn. Let's apply these principles into an action plan and get started. Are you ready to leave your mark on the world? Let's do this!

COMMUNITY PROJECT WORKBOOK

Plan Your Own Community Project

This workbook will help you turn your passion into a meaningful community project and make a difference!

Step 1: Live from your passion. Passion fuels your purpose and inspires others to join you. What are you passionate about? Is it the environment, helping others, social justice, animal welfare, or something else? Think about what excites you and drives you to take action.

What are your passions? Write them below:

_____
_____
_____
_____
_____

Brainstorm: How could you turn one of your passions into something that makes a difference in your community?

_____
_____
_____
_____
_____

Step 2: Find the gap. What needs in your local community, school, or neighborhood align with your passion? Look around your community. What could be improved? Where is there a gap or need your passion could help fill?

Identify the gap:

_____
_____
_____
_____
_____

Step 3: Set goals. Your goals can be big or small, but every step you take brings you closer to making an impact. Now that you've identified your passion and the gap you want to address, think about what you want to achieve. Set clear, actionable goals for your project.

Examples of goals:

- Clean up a local park.
- Raise $500 for charity.
- Organize a food drive for families in need.

Write your goals below:

_____
_____
_____
_____
_____

Step 4: Set yourself up for success. Who will you need to help you? What tools or supplies will you need? Do you need to call anyone to ask permission or get an adult to support your endeavor? What steps do you need to take to make this happen? No leader works alone. Think about the tools, organizations, supplies, and people who can support you in bringing your project to life. Create a list. Maybe it's friends, family, classmates, teachers, or community members.

List the people you'll ask for help:

1. _____
2. _____
3. _____
4. _____
5. _____

Step 5: Create a plan. Create a step-by-step action plan to help you complete your mission. For example, your first step might be gathering supplies.

Outline the steps you'll take to complete your project:

1. _____
2. _____
3. _____
4. _____
5. _____
6. _____
7. _____
8. _____

Step 6: Take action. Remember that actions speak louder than words. Take the first step and stay focused on your goals. Even small actions can create big change. Choose a date and location, then take the first step to bring your plan to life!

What will your first step be?

_____
_____
_____
_____
_____

Step 7: Inspire others. Leadership isn't just about doing; it's about motivating others to join your cause. Share your vision with others. Talk about why this project matters to you and why it's important for your community. Invite others to join your cause and be part of the difference you're making.

Who can you inspire to join you?

_____
_____
_____
_____
_____

How will you share your vision (social media, school announcements, word of mouth, etc.)?

_____
_____
_____
_____
_____

Step 8: Leave a legacy. Consider how your efforts can create lasting change, even after your project is done. Reflect on how your project will continue to make an impact. Could it inspire someone else to start a similar project? Will it lead to lasting improvements in your community? Is there someone you know who would love to be a part of your project?

What legacy do you want to leave behind?

Reflection Section

After completing your project, take some time to reflect:

What difference did your project make in your community?

How did it feel to lead this project?

What did you learn about yourself and leadership?

What changes would you make for your next project?

Final Thoughts

You have the power to create change. By living from your passion, finding the gap, and taking action, you can inspire others and leave a lasting legacy by contributing to your community. Every step you take builds your leadership and creates a better world—and you get to have fun in the process.

What's your next big idea? Start dreaming, planning, and making it happen. You've got this!

CHAPTER 10

YOUR LEADERSHIP ADVENTURE

Put It All Together: Create Your Personal Leadership Plan
By Corri Evans

You've reached the last chapter. How do you *feel?*

As you close this book, remember that leadership is not just about absorbing inspiring stories or mastering new skills; it's about translating vision into action. That's why crafting a personalized leadership plan is the crucial next step. This plan serves as your North Star, guiding you to clarify your purpose, focus your efforts, and chart a roadmap for growth. Committing your goals to paper, tracking progress, and holding yourself accountable will transform inspiration into tangible, life-changing results.

Over the next ten weeks, embark on a transformative journey to create your leadership plan. Begin by reflecting on your why—the heartbeat of your leadership (weeks one and two). Uncover your core values, leadership philosophy, and the principles that drive you. What ignites your passion? What kind of leader do you aspire to be?

Next, define and write your short-term and long-term goals (weeks three and four). Break down big dreams into manageable objectives, ensuring each step aligns with your vision. Identify the skills, knowledge, and relationships necessary to achieve these goals.

Develop a detailed action plan with specific steps, timelines, and milestones (weeks five and six). Consider potential obstacles and contingency plans.

Create a progress tracking system and accountability structure (weeks seven and eight), leveraging tools like journals, spreadsheets, or mentorship.

Finally, review, revise, and finalize your plan (weeks nine and ten). Regularly assess your progress, celebrate successes, and adjust your course as needed. Remember, this is your unique journey—be patient, flexible, and kind to yourself throughout the process.

Don't be afraid to seek feedback and guidance from trusted mentors, peers, or role models. Surround yourself with a supportive community that believes in your potential. Most importantly, take consistent, bold action; your leadership plan is only as effective as the progress you make.

By putting these principles into practice, you'll become the leader you've always envisioned—confident, compassionate, and capable of inspiring positive change. Congratulations, leader; your journey starts now!

Your Leadership Adventure
Keep Growing, Never Stop Improving
By Juli Hughes

As a trailblazing teen leader, you're about to discover a game-changing truth: Growth is a lifelong journey, not a destination. Reaching milestones and achieving goals is just the beginning; it's where the real growth accelerates. The moment you think you've "arrived" is when you start stagnating, losing momentum and relevance. You get to commit to continuous learning, self-improvement, and evolution to stay ahead of the curve and leave a lasting impact.

Think of yourself as a dynamic, ever-growing tree. With each new experience, your roots deepen, and your branches strengthen. However, if you stop growing, you'll wither away, vulnerable to the unpredictable winds of change. By embracing a growth mindset, you'll remain flexible, adaptable, and resilient in the face of challenges.

So, how do you fuel this growth? Seek feedback from others; it takes courage, but it's the ultimate catalyst for growth. Devour books, articles, and fresh perspectives. Attend workshops, webinars, and conferences that spark new ideas. Find a mentor who'll guide and challenge you. Take calculated risks and try novel approaches. That's where the magic unfolds.

Remember, growth is a daily journey, not a distant destination. The small, consistent actions add up to make a monumental difference. Stay insatiably curious, keep learning, and never stop refining your leadership craft. You're capable of incredible impact!

And when setbacks inevitably arise—because they will—don't quit. Instead, harness them as opportunities to learn, adapt, and surge forward. Every failure is a steppingstone to success, and every success is a chance to refine and improve. Keep pushing yourself to be better, do better, and lead better.

The world urgently needs your unique brand of leadership, and it's counting on you to keep growing, improving, and innovating every step of the way. Your leadership journey is a marathon, not a sprint. Pace yourself, stay focused, and never lose sight of your vision. The newest, most extraordinary version of yourself is waiting to emerge. Keep growing, and you'll unleash a leadership legacy that transforms lives.

Celebrate Your Wins and Set New Goals
By Corri Evans and Juli Hughes

As you pause to celebrate your wins and reflect on your remarkable journey, take a moment to acknowledge the profound impact you've made thus far. Consider the ripple effects of your leadership, the lives you've touched, and the challenges you've overcome. Ask yourself: What skills or knowledge can I acquire to propel my leadership to new heights? How can I harness my successes to empower and inspire others, creating a wave of positive change that resonates far beyond my accomplishments?

Celebrate your wins, no matter how small they may seem. Treat yourself to a favorite meal or activity, share your achievements with loved ones, or write them in a triumph journal. Create a "Wall of Wins" where you post notes or mementos from each success. Reflect on the journey, not just the destination, and acknowledge the growth, resilience, and determination that have carried you this far.

As you bask in the glory of your achievements, remember that true leadership is about leveraging success to elevate others and drive meaningful progress. Use your wins as a springboard for growth and innovation, asking yourself:

- What's the next frontier for me as a leader?
- How can I disrupt the status quo and bring fresh ideas to the table?
- What's one thing I can do differently to make a more significant impact?
- How can I harness my influence to create positive change?

Tracking your results can help you stay focused and motivated, but beware of getting too caught up in metrics. Instead, use your progress as a neutral reflection tool, allowing yourself to reset and adjust course when needed. Regularly ask yourself:

- What's working?
- What's not?
- What adjustments can I make to stay on track?

By embracing this growth mindset, you'll ensure your successes become the foundation for even greater achievements.

Ultimately, the true measure of your leadership lies not in your accomplishments but in the lasting impact you create. So, take a moment to revel in your successes, then ask yourself the tough questions that will propel you to even greater heights. What will you do with your success? Will you simply enjoy it or use it as fuel to change the world? The choice is yours.

You've Read this *Amazing* Book! Now What? Embracing Your Authentic Leadership
By Corri Evans

As you stand at the threshold of your leadership journey, remember that you are exactly who you're meant to be in this very moment. Your unique blend of experiences, passions, and talents has forged a powerful leader ready to ignite positive change in the world. It's time to unlock the full potential of your authentic self, embracing the strengths, values, and vision that make you unstoppable.

Begin by reflecting on your core values—the non-negotiable principles that drive, inspire, and guide your decisions. You have identified the compass that navigates your life's journey. Continue to ask yourself:

What do I stand for, and what do I refuse to compromise on?

As you identify your strengths, those brilliant skills and talents that shine the brightest, let them illuminate your path. Envision the leadership impact you want to create—the ripple effect of positivity, the transformative power of your presence. Craft a clear and concise vision statement that captures the essence of the change you want to make, and let it serve as your North Star.

From this foundation, set specific, measurable, achievable, relevant, and time-bound goals that propel you toward your vision. Break free from the limitations of self-doubt and fear, and instead, tap into your inner reservoir of resilience and determination. Consider who you want to inspire and influence—your target audience—and craft a communication strategy that resonates with them, speaking directly to their hearts and minds. Plan for personal growth, develop skills, seek feedback, and learn from setbacks, knowing that every experience is an opportunity to refine your leadership edge.

Create an action plan, outlining deliberate steps toward your goals, and identify the resources and support you need to succeed. Surround yourself with mentors, allies, and a community that believes in your vision. Regularly review and revise your progress, celebrating successes and adapting to new opportunities. And when the journey gets tough, draw upon your inner strength, remembering that every great leader has faced uncertainty and overcome adversity.

This journey is yours to own, and your vision will guide your next steps as a leader in your life, family, community, and the world around you. You are the architect of your destiny, the catalyst for transformation. Congratulations, you're now ready to embark on the next chapter of your life, marked by purpose, passion, and profound impact. Begin now and create the vision your heart desires. The world is waiting.

MY LEADERSHIP PLEDGE

This pledge is a commitment to myself, my growth, and my leadership journey.

By signing this, I promise to hold myself accountable for my growth and actions and to embody the leader I aspire to be.

I _____, pledge to:

Have a clear vision for the leader I want to be.

Lead with integrity, authenticity, and kindness.

Take ownership of my choices and actions.

View obstacles as opportunities for growth.

Develop self-awareness, empathy, and resilience.

Support and uplift others in their journey.

Pursue my goals and dreams with purpose and determination.

Signature: _____

Date: _____

This personal leadership pledge is a reminder of my commitment to continue discovering the leader in me.

ABOUT THE AUTHORS

Imagine a world of love, courage, authenticity, and freedom.

As children, we naturally seek connection, playing games like tag, hide-and-seek, or building pillow forts. As teenagers, we find our place within circles of friends, forming communities where we belong. And sometimes, as adults, we get the extraordinary opportunity to come together as a team with a powerful mission to make an impact. That's where your authors come in.

We are a team of global leaders united by a shared mission to empower the next generation. We are the *Committed Visionaries*—**a diverse group of twenty-three individuals with unique backgrounds, experiences, and perspectives united by one common vision: to create a world of love, courage, authenticity, and freedom.**

We are a dynamic group of devoted students, children, and parents navigating leadership in our everyday lives. Our team includes successful entrepreneurs, published authors, compassionate healthcare professionals, and changemakers from different parts of the world. Some of us have built businesses or developed communities, and some have track records of guiding teams and organizations. Leadership is at the heart of everything we do and who we are.

Our shared dream is to inspire transformation and cultivate leadership in others. Drawing from our collective experiences, we noticed a gap in leadership guides and resources for young people and decided to fill it.

This book is part of that dream—a collaboration born from our commitment to work together and empower youth to pursue their dreams.

We want to inspire a new wave of compassionate, courageous, and innovative leaders who will positively influence and impact their friendships, families, schools, communities, and the world.

We created a comprehensive resource that equips teenagers with the skills, confidence, and resilience to thrive.

We aim specifically for those of you in your teenage years, in a stage of discovery and growth—a time when your circle of friends becomes your community and shapes your identity. We believe you were born to lead, and we want to guide you as you choose to step into leadership.

Many people dream, but few experience their dreams coming true. Fewer still have the courage to consciously create them. That's where you come in.

We trust this book will inspire you to take that step—to dream boldly, lead courageously, and create meaningful change in the world around you.

Our Commitment to You

We, the Committed Visionaries, created this book, *Leadership for Teens: Discover the Leader in YOU*, from the lessons we have learned along our leadership journey, and from our combined years of life experiences.

In this book, we provide practical tools, real-life examples, inspiring stories, and effective strategies to support your leadership skills, personal growth, and character development. It is our hope that these insights spark meaningful change in your life and empower you to lead with confidence and purpose.

Beyond this Book

Leadership is more than a set of skills. It is a way of being! We invite you to continue in this discovery adventure, so you can powerfully embrace your role as one of the leaders who is shaping the future with courage, authenticity, and purpose. Together, we can create a brighter tomorrow starting today. We are here to support YOU and your Vision!

For more information and updates about the Committed Visionaries, visit us at www.committedvisionaries.com.

The Gift of Life

In a world where it's easy to feel unseen, baby Elijah reminds us that every life carries infinite beauty and meaning, no matter how brief. Elijah is the son of Keia Lavine, a cherished co-author of this book. Let the gift of life awaken hearts, spark a movement, and change the world.

Life is precious.

Life is NOW!

Printed in Dunstable, United Kingdom

64629070R00084